THE ACADEMIC COACH

How To Create a High Performance Culture in Higher Education Using Data-Driven Leadership

Richard Hill, PhD

Copyright © 2016 G. R. Hill

All rights reserved.

ISBN-13: 9781520723129

DEDICATION

To absent friends who taught me a lot during their lives,
and even more since their passing.

CONTENTS

	Acknowledgements	viii
1	Preface	Pg 1
	Part One	Pg 7
2	Introduction	Pg 8
3	Performance Management	Pg 12
4	Coaching	Pg 20
5	The Coaching Manager	Pg 28
6	Data-driven	Pg 35
	Part Two	Pg 41
7	ADVANCE Overview	Pg 42
8	Strategy – Awareness	Pg 53
9	Strategy – Definition	Pg 78
10	Strategy – Vision	Pg 84
11	Tactics – Analytics	Pg 100
12	Tactics – Navigate	Pg 113

13	Tactics – Cultivate	Pg 121
14	Tactics – Externalise	Pg 136
	Part Three	Pg 145
15	Additional Resources	Pg 146
16	Wrap-up	Pg 162

ACKNOWLEDGEMENTS

Of course, books like these inevitably are influenced by many of the people that we work with over the years. However, I would like to thank a few who have directly contributed to my experience and thinking in this area:

Nick Antonopoulos, Sue Beckingham, Neale Birch, Grant Evans, Dave Lees, Ranald MacDonald, David Moore, Siavash Moshiri and Kim Smith.

PREFACE

Whilst it can sometimes feel that managing academic staff is like 'herding cats', it needn't always be the case. Academics often resist management. But they love to be led. How can you become a steward of change?

Whether you are new to academic management or you are more experienced, *The Academic Coach* will show you how to:

- Use a framework of tools to identify strategic and tactical objectives;

- Empower staff to utilise data to make great decisions;

- Support academic staff through periods of change;

- Create a high-performance culture;

- Help staff make life-changing decisions to accelerate their careers;

- Overcome limiting beliefs for yourself and others;

- Re-profile staff skills to balance teaching, research and income generation;

- Realise the full potential of staff in higher education environments.

Intended audience

This book will help you explore the use of evidence-based coaching skills in the academic environment, so that you can achieve more success in your role. The audience of this book is likely to include:

- Academic and administrative managers such as Subject/Section/Team Leaders and Heads of School/Department;

- Executive team members such as Deans, Associate/Assistant Deans and Pro-vice Chancellors;

- Leadership roles without line management responsibilities such as School/Department/Faculty Teaching Fellows, Quality Enhancement Leads, Heads of Student Experience and similar;

- Those with academic responsibilities for teaching such as Module/Programme/Course Leaders;

- Staff who aspire to leadership roles, who want to develop greater powers of influence.

If you are in a position where you need to turn-around the performance of an academic department, to meet the increased pressures of the external Higher Education environment, then you will need to know how to:

- Increase the department's self-awareness;

- Position your department in relation to the competition;

- Create a compelling vision for change;

- Identify relevant key performance measures;

- Leverage institutional resources for tangible improvements;

- Cultivate a culture of enquiry;

- Create and exploit a departmental brand.

Whilst the example of a department has been given, any other entity such as a team, school or individual is also applicable.

The approach described in this book has been used successfully with both individuals and groups of staff. So, your list of requirements might alternatively look like this:

- Increase your self-awareness;

- Position yourself in relation to future roles;

- Create a compelling vision for your own development;

- Identify relevant key performance measures of your success;

- Leverage resources for self-improvement;

- Cultivate a culture of enquiry around you;
- Create and exploit your personal brand.

Whether you are developing yourself, an individual, a group of individuals or an organisation, the foundations of this book are the same. We'll use a combination of fact-based data capture, alongside appropriate coaching skills, to develop a blueprint for a high performance culture.

How to use this book

Like many books of this type, the maximum value is realised when you use the information to experiment and then build upon your own experience.

In the first instance, read the book from start to finish. If you have prior experience in a particular area you can skip some pages and read ahead.

It's important to observe the sequence and see where each element fits into the overall picture. Once you have an overview, you can then dip into chapters as and when required.

Along the way, there are lots of prompts to reflect, try things out and evaluate the results; use these prompts to pause and relate what you have read, to what you have experienced.

Talking about a topic often deepens our understanding, so make good use of your circles of colleagues and friends. When it comes to the deeper more personal reflection, it is vital to have an objective, external view from a trusted party.

Above all, it's important to be *optimistic* and *enthusiastic* when developing ourselves and those around us. As leaders we should be *inspirational*, *generous*, *forgiving*, *supportive* and *set an example* for our followers.

Adopting these principles (with the help of some simple tools) will empower you to face challenges head-on and achieve your real potential.

About this book

This book is organised into three parts as follows:

- *Part One* provides an overview of the challenges and context within which we work. It also provides some working definitions of what it means to coach in the workplace, as well as exploring the concept of performance management in the HE environment. You'll gather evidence and increase your self-awareness to strengthen your academic leadership.

- *Part Two* describes ADVANCE, a model for personal and organisational transformation. ADVANCE is composed of two phases, strategy and tactics, to help structure and formulate the rigorous use of data to inform your leadership of development activities.

- *Part Three* provides some additional resources to use alongside ADVANCE on your improvement journey.

Throughout the book there are exercises to prompt your thinking and promote deeper understanding. I have included exercises that have been particularly revealing for both myself and those I have coached.

One advantage of having a book pose a challenging

question, rather than a colleague or your line manager, is that you don't have to tell anyone the answer if you are not quite ready to confess!

However, I recommend that you write your answers down. One of the difficulties of personal development is that we forget what it was like not to know.

Writing down your current thinking provides some facts upon which we can reflect at a later date, which helps us understand to what extent we have changed. This, in itself is a liberating and motivating habit to develop.

Above all this book is about change.

And change starts from within.

PART ONE

Part One introduces the Higher Education context and explores performance management, coaching and the importance of data-driven academic leadership.

2 INTRODUCTION

The Higher Education context

Higher Education in the United Kingdom is changing at an unprecedented rate. Changes in government policy have resulted first in the creation of a quasi-market by introducing student fees, prior to the transition to a competitive free market whereby Student Number Control (SNC) quotas were removed in 2014.

Higher Education Institutions (HEI) now compete with each other for fee-paying students, rather than receiving funding from the Higher Education Funding Councils. At the time of writing (2016), the fee that can be charged is capped; it is anticipated that this control may also be relaxed in the future, enabling price differentiation to occur between HEIs as well.

This move towards a more commercial marketplace demands more service-oriented behaviours, and just like private industries, the HEI organisational activities will be held to account in terms of financial sustainability.

Systems and processes will come under pressure to be leaner, and the measurement and improvement of performance will be a focus of organisational decision-making.

Whilst performance measurement and management have always been a core part of corporate business at all levels, this concept is relatively new to the academic functions within HEIs.

Traditionally, HEIs have built reputations upon research and teaching quality, and the 'attractiveness' of other qualitative characteristics such as the facilities and desirability of the host city. As such, the internal cultures within HEIs have evolved to reflect this thinking, and so the consideration of 'performance' (which is broadly measured externally by league tables) has been a relatively alien concept. As the marketplace emerges, performance will be on an equal footing with reputation.

The challenge

When the environment changes, those entities within it have to respond with their own change. Universities are no different and HEI management must successfully navigate the transition from being a publicly funded body to a corporate institution.

What does that mean for the administrative, teaching and research staff, who are focused upon delivering the educational experience?

It usually means 'change initiatives', 'working parties', 'task and finish groups' and a whole host of activities that either modify, delete or introduce processes and systems. In fact, there are large bodies of literature on topics such as 'Business Process Re-engineering' and the like, as methods and approaches to successfully achieving change.

However, I will posit that the key to performance improvement lies not within processes and systems. It's all about the *people*.

How many change projects have forged ahead towards an outcome, with team members privately forecasting a disaster?

How many committees have collectively embedded organisational change that actually reduces the performance of an institution?

How many student-centred systems are serving the needs of the university, rather than the student?

The leanest, most practical and sensible solution to a challenge typically lies closest to the source of the problem. Our key challenge is to help foster a culture where the environment is agile and receptive to positive change. A culture where staff feel empowered to be accountable, and they possess the capability to provide solutions.

Such an environment is not developed via more bureaucracy. Since bureaucracy is embedded in HEIs there is a lot of work to do. But, before we get started we should explore what performance management means.

Exercise

Take a moment to think about what performance management means to you. You may have some experience of it from another industry, or you might have been involved in it in your current role. If you have no experience, then think about what it might mean in your present context.

Once you have reflected for a short while, write down some responses to the following prompt questions:

- What does the term 'performance management' conjure up in your mind?

- What scenarios at work do you think would be improved by the use of performance management?

- Do you feel that performance management is a positive phrase? If not, what are your reasons for thinking otherwise?

Keep your responses to hand for the next chapter (3).

As I mentioned earlier, such an exercise can be a good record to help you gauge your progress in the future. To help with this, record the date that you answered the questions and file them somewhere safe.

3 PERFORMANCE MANAGEMENT

What is performance management?

I think that it's fair to say that if you hear 'performance management' in an academic context, then it is referring to a negative situation. People tend to be 'performance managed' when their behaviour or ability to perform a role is under question.

The connotation is that staff from the Human Resource (HR) department will be involved, and that some formal processes will be underway. So, performance management can be perceived as something that is *done* to staff when they are not measuring up to a standard.

> **Reflection:** *How does this compare with your answers to the previous exercise?*

Perhaps though, performance management should not be exclusive to dealing with situations of poor performance. It should reflect the approaches employed to manage performance at all levels, both good and not-so-good.

Of course, some would argue that the role of a university is far too complex to boil down into a few quantitative measures, and any attempt to specify measures to be managed, will result in added tension when the monitoring systems are implemented.

For instance, the breadth of activities that a university undertakes will inevitably lead to compromises being made. Maximising excellence in research has to be made at the expense of other activities.

Such activities can differ between HEIs; the ability to maintain good student satisfaction scores, or the amount of industrial ('third-stream') income are likely suffer if the academic staff focus wholly upon high-quality journal articles.

Conversely, an enterprising university may find that its entrepreneurial income generation may be constraining an ability to create new knowledge and solicit research council funding.

And of course, a focus upon income generation through student tuition fees may create a culture that finds it difficult to relate to the wider benefits of engaging in research and scholarly activity.

In all cases there are tensions that require sensitive management. We should remember though, that what might be a complex situation for a group of staff (such as a department), might actually be distilled down to something that is much more polarised for an individual member of staff.

For instance, a department may strategically plan to change its income profile to increase the proportion of funded research.

Whilst for a research active academic this could reinforce or amplify the tension between teaching and research duties, for a teaching-oriented academic there may be no foreseeable change in their immediate future.

> **Reflection:** *Think back to your last appraisal meeting with your line manager. What aspects of that discussion, in relation to your performance, were, or could be, counter-productive for you?*

Our understanding of performance management is shaped by our experiences of being managed in an academic context. It is not uncommon for first time academic line managers to be exasperated by annual appraisal discussions with academic staff.

Some staff will enthusiastically discuss quantifiable targets for the year ahead, and offer an insightful commentary on their performance for the previous year.

Others will appear noncommittal and defensive; they'll describe their contribution as strong but argue that their work is necessarily complex and unable to be measured.

Another academic may provide an outright objection to the whole process and provide the basis of 'a difficult conversation', and in some cases cite the measurement of performance as a contributor to poor personal well-being.

The mixture of these discussions will vary depending upon the prevalent culture of the institution, but also the local culture within departments and teams.

It is useful to consider how this culture might be fostered by the predominant approach to management in your environment.

Directive or self-directed management?

A directive approach to management typically exhibits the following characteristics:

- Performance measures and goals and determined at all levels of the institution, and formulated by the senior leadership team;

- Managers monitor the performance of individuals against local targets;

- Your line manager makes it clear what has to be done, how it should be done and by when;

- Performance is assessed in terms of how well the work was done;

- Frequent use of initiatives/project working to achieve short term goals.

In terms of the daily conversations, a directive manager would have a tendency to instruct:

- *"That's the second year running that the assessment and feedback scores have been less than 60%. You need to investigate and report back with an action plan by next Tuesday."*

- *"Those application conversion figures don't add up. Marketing don't seem to be able to talk to Central Planning."*

- *"The Quality Lead won't like this. Get support from Central Intelligence and Estates first, before you present a paper at the Committee meeting."*

This style is motivated by outcomes and can be frequently encountered in academic support/administrative areas. It also occurs in academic areas to varying degrees.

In contrast there is management that encourages staff to be *self-directed*.

This can be characterised as:

- The mission of the organisation is identified, with the declaration of long-term ambitions;

- A series of stakeholder consultations are held to determine the strategic priorities;

- Action plans are created that may include qualitative and vague outcomes;

- Managers utilise measures to initiate discussions around enhancement;

- Managers use the mission to reinforce what has to be achieved, and refer to assessments of values and behaviours as measures of progress;

- Significant emphasis is placed upon the staff recruitment processes, to ensure that incoming staff are of an appropriate 'fit'.

The daily dialogue also reflects the increased focus upon the individual, rather than on a system or process:

- *"I've seen the assessment and feedback scores as well. What do you think is the cause?"*

- *"The application figures seem to regularly have errors in them. What are the reasons for this happening?"*

- *"I think we can see where this is heading. How would you tackle it?"*

A self-directed style of management encourages a greater alignment between the intrinsic motivation of an individual and the organisation, with less reliance upon the control and reporting of performance against short term objectives.

Traditionally, this represents the stereotypical academic environment, whereby academic staff are trusted to work to support the institution's mission, rather than to perform in a coordinated way to achieve an end of year operating surplus.

Managers that require specific objectives to be met in a short timeframe can find this situation particularly frustrating. However, the emerging competitive marketplace in HE has started to focus the minds of university executive leaders in such a way that HEIs are starting to adopt more directive styles of management.

In the same way that managers can be frustrated with a department of self-directed academic staff, academics can also find directives and 'managerialism' problematic.

Like most things in life it is a question of balance; where the balance lies is likely to be different for each institution. But the increased pressure to perform well both financially and in the published league tables, combined with the potentially destructive situation of failing to get the best out of academic staff, means that there is much to gain or lose depending upon the approaches we adopt as leaders.

It's important that we make sufficient effort to understand our environment so that we can devise the best approach. You might think that a book that advocates the use of data to achieve transformation might be heading down the road of directive management.

But data is not always quantifiable in the sense of ratios or absolute numbers, and qualitative data is often a rich source of insight for the curious.

If we are to be successful at managing performance, we have to appreciate what is worth measuring, what will motivate individuals, and how they respond to the local culture.

In subsequent chapters we shall explore a framework that will help determine the most appropriate way forward for a transformation; remember that the transformation can be ourselves, another individual, or a group of people.

But before we get there, we shall explore how behaviour, and particular changes in behaviour, can assist the rate at which significant transformations can be made.

Exercise

Take some time to reflect upon the prompt questions below. Don't forget to write down your responses.

- Who sets the mission and strategic objectives of your institution? Who should do this?

- Are measures used to assess performance or are they used as a catalyst for discussions around enhancement? What questions are likely to be raised during your own appraisal review?

- Do you feel that your line manager makes decisions based on the university mission, even if it means that an improvement cannot be measured quantitatively?

- During the recruitment of new staff, is there an assessment made with regard to the candidate's values and beliefs?

- Does the management invest resources in new systems and processes, or in the development of individuals?

4 COACHING

What is coaching?

For a long time the practice of 'coaching' has been associated with sport, and more specifically it refers to a role whereby a 'coach' assists a 'coachee' to improve their competitive performance. The coach offers an external perspective of the coachee, and can utilise this position to help diagnose barriers to improved performance.

Over time the practice of coaching has become synonymous with enhancing performance in a much wider set of situations, such as business or personal coaching. If we consider 'coach' as a noun, we see that it refers to a carriage that transports people from one place to another.

In the context of improving performance, coaching is a means of taking someone from one state and transporting them towards a different, enhanced state.

It is common for senior business leaders to employ personal coaches. These coaches can observe their clients and offer an unbiased challenge that is free from organisational politics. The coach offers a confidential space for the executive to explore current challenges, and is a focused listener with which to work through potential solutions.

As individuals face greater challenges in the workplace, and the focus of continuous, personal development becomes more pervasive, greater numbers of people outside of executive management are recruiting personal coaches.

So what is coaching? At its heart, coaching can be as simple as one conversation. It is the type of conversation where two people interact and the focus is positive and centred on one of the parties only (the coachee). The other party (the coach) challenges the coachee in a way that makes them think deeper about their challenges, so that they can reflect afterwards, learn more about themselves, and develop their own solution.

Coaching is not about instruction, nor is it about offering specific advice. It is about the use of language to challenge a coachee's thinking processes in order to help them learn and develop. If the coaching mindset is developed, the single coaching conversation becomes a constant stream of conversations that encourages coachees to become more empowered in their actions, and to take the initiative more frequently.

Using and practicing skills such as listening, questioning, reflection and feedback enables coaches to challenge their coachees to develop without explicitly directing them. This 'non-directive' approach is the basis of a coaching mindset.

Having an awareness of coaching opens up an inordinate number of potential coaching opportunities.

You might be standing in a queue for coffee with someone; you could be seizing 30 seconds in a corridor; you might be using powerful questions in a team or departmental meeting; or you might have requested a formal meeting to explore a particular situation in a deeper way.

All of these situations present opportunities to coach and therefore, these are all opportunities to enhance performance.

The benefits don't stop with the coach though. Those who adopt the coaching mindset find that they become more influential in the workplace and they posses a better understanding of the workplace culture. But perhaps most importantly they learn a lot about themselves through the practice of coaching others.

This enhanced self-awareness is very powerful.

So to summarise, a coaching conversation has the following characteristics:

- The focus of the conversation is the learning and progress of an individual;

- A coach uses 'non-directive' approaches by practicing listening, questioning and feedback skills;

- The coachee will be challenged such that they reflect more deeply after the conversation and experience personal growth as a result.

These characteristics have no bearing on the location or length of a conversation.

Even an acknowledgement in the car park, first thing in the morning, is an opportunity to coach!

Why coaching for academia?

So far, we have established a few things. First, the HE environment is changing into a competitive marketplace. Whilst the complexity of services that a university offers has not necessarily changed, the emphasis upon the achievement of short term outcomes is greater than has been traditionally the case.

Second, the desire to be regarded as competitive has added weight to discussions around performance measurement and the management of performance. The complexity of most HEIs means that there are particular functions where performance has been actively monitored, but generally the concept of 'performance management' is seen as a remedial activity for staff that are incapable.

Third, the effect of working towards longer term aims or 'a mission' has guided the evolution of cultures that can find short term objectives an irrelevance. As such, the focus of management has tended to favour people over processes for academic staff, in contrast with more directive styles for administrative/professional services staff.

These three factors are not an exhaustive list, but they do give a flavour of the overall challenge. If universities are to change, our leadership needs to successfully chart a path that attempts to optimise the performance of the individual/team/organisation as a whole.

Coaching and learning

Universities are in the business of learning. Not as

narrowly defined as a pure training organisation (although many HEIs sell training as part of their portfolio of offerings), but to sustainably provide education now and in the future, is a fundamental principle.

As such, a HEI's 'core business' is learning, whether it be through student tuition, research or industrial income generation. Another perspective is that organisations that are sustainable in the long term have to be able to adapt, and therefore have the capacity to learn; even the more modern HEIs have been established longer than a lot of private businesses. Certainly the traditional universities have substantial histories spanning several centuries.

However, anyone who has worked in a HEI for a significant period will have witnessed the same mistakes repeated time after time. What does this say about the HEI as a learning organisation?

> **Reflection:** *Remember a time when you foresaw a mistake being repeated. Write down the key characteristics of the weakness and describe the end result. What specific conditions need to change for the organisation to learn for the future?*

And so we return to coaching. At the heart of coaching is development, or learning. From earlier:

"… coaching can be as simple as one conversation. It is the type of conversation where two people interact and the focus is positive and centred on one of the parties only (the coachee). The other party (the coach) challenges the coachee in a way that makes them think deeper about their challenges, so that they can reflect afterwards, learn more about themselves, and develop their own solution."

If the environment is conducive to coaching then it will be acceptable to approach your line manager to discuss your own performance, particularly because you want it to improve. You'll do this knowing that your manager will genuinely want to support you without recording it as a deficit in your next appraisal.

The conversation (or series of conversations) will challenge you to think, learn, and derive your own solution, which will increase your personal capability.

From your line manager's perspective there are some significant benefits of a coaching-friendly environment.

First, staff that approach you with the expectation of a coaching conversation will reveal more to you about their overall interest for work. As a result you will understand them better, what motivates them, and what development they are seeking.

Second, you will have a deeper understanding of what they can achieve and your trust in their capabilities will increase. You'll know which activities they can complete successfully, but you'll also have the confidence that their learning mindset will prevent them from repeating mistakes. In terms of performance monitoring you'll have greater confidence in their abilities than looking at a spreadsheet of numbers.

Third, staff who are self-directed demand less time from their managers. You'll spend less time fixing every problem yourself and more time building an organisation that can adapt to environmental changes.

Fourth, a coaching style of management reinforces autonomous learning amongst staff. Whilst we can't necessarily insulate every academic from short term objectives and management directives, a coaching culture can prevent the need to be directive for most of the time.

Coaching language

Since coaching utilises conversation, a fundamental part of successful coaching is our use of language.

Coaching is about challenging conversations and therefore an important skill is building a repertoire of questions that will challenge a coachee sufficiently.

One basic principle of coaching is to resist the asking of *closed* questions. Closed questions result in a 'yes' or 'no' answer. Here are some examples:

- *"Is there a way of improving the student attendance in your lectures?"*

- *"Do you know why the applicant conversion rate has dropped?"*

- *"Can you see that working?"*

- *"Do you have any other options other than scaling the marks up?"*

The issue with closed questions is that the conversation is shut down there and then. All the recipient has to do is answer "yes" or "no".

Of course we would normally follow up with another question, but this results in an interrogation, which is one-sided against the coachee, rather than a conversation where there is more parity.

So, let's see what these closed questions might look like with some simple modifications:

- *"What can you do to improve the student attendance in*

your lectures?"

- *"What are the reasons for the applicant conversion rate dropping?"*

- *"How can you see that working?"*

- *"What options do you have?"*

The closed questions are now *open*. They set the scene for a range of answers, which the coachee is now challenged to explore. When you feel a closed question forming in your mind, rework it to commence with 'what', 'where', 'when', 'who' or 'how' and it won't close the conversation down.

This is a simple technique that can significantly increase the value of your interactions with staff. Using open questions means that the 30 second interaction in the corridor can now be part of a legitimate coaching approach.

You can also start small - in the next committee meeting - and look for the benefits, without overtly advertising that you have recently read a book and changed your management style!

Exercise

Start immediately! Commit to using open questions in your next conversation and observe the results. For the first few interactions, record some notes afterwards about the essence of the conversation, the open question/s you used, and the results obtained.

You may be surprised at the difference that language can make.

5 THE COACHING MANAGER

Coaching and management

Coaching is a popular topic, particularly in the world of business. Executive leaders employ personal coaches to have developmental conversations, to explore hypothetical scenarios, and to encourage self-awareness. It follows that the practice has expanded, with many people deciding to make careers of coaching, as greater numbers of individuals use coaching services to improve their own development.

One of the defining aspects of business/life/personal coaching is the absolute focus upon the *processes* of coaching. The coaching engagements are typically short term, perhaps six separate sessions for instance, and therefore there is a lot of emphasis on developing techniques to establish 'rapport' quickly between the client and the coach.

Coaches that focus on helping clients solve their own challenges need not know anything about a particular business domain or industry; in fact the fresh perspective may be a significant advantage in terms of lateral thinking. In addition, each engagement is clearly identified - the session will be dedicated to coaching - with no chance of conversations being polluted by the most recent managerial crisis.

Such coaches practice the skills of coaching conversation, using powerful questions to challenge and pursue potential barriers in the client's thinking. The conversation may be augmented with specific tools that can help clients gain a new outlook on a situation.

What these coaches don't have therefore, is a line management responsibility for the client. In fact, they are *employed* by the client so there is a relationship of *service*.

The coach is not required to appraise the client with a view to determining any actions other than to improve the client's performance.

Finally, the coach has a defined engagement with the client that is usually temporary in nature. Once the required development has been undertaken, the relationship ceases.

In sharp contrast, the coaching manager has a line management responsibility for the coachee. They are required to appraise the coachee at least annually, and the outcome of that appraisal may be linked to career progression.

In addition, the relationship normally is expected to be of a more significant length.

With these characteristics in place, how does this affect the manager's ability to coach?

> **Reflection:** *Think beyond the use of open questions in your dialogue with staff. What difficulties might you envisage if you adopt a more developmental approach towards your staff?*

It's important to realise that a coaching manager has to adopt a different outlook to a 'pure' coach. Coaching practice is different to having the responsibility for staff and operations. Tasks have to be completed on time and to the correct standard, in an efficient manner.

There is bound to be directive language in the requisite conversations, otherwise the short term objectives might not be met.

In terms of the annual appraisal, or any event where a manager has to evaluate the performance of a member of staff (which is more common in project-oriented environments), there is a fundamental tension between making judgements (appraising) and coaching.

When we appraise staff, we are placing the focus upon the objectives of the organisation, rather than the needs of the individual.

As we have discussed so far, whilst coaching could be the preferred way of supporting the development of individuals, it can only at best follow on from an appraisal.

The fact that an appraisal conversation can be less conducive to coaching, means that the coaching manager would be wise to clearly identify the context of the discussion up front.

So, be clear when you are making organisational judgements based on the needs of the institution, and be clear when you are coaching.

Developing a coaching mindset

The decision to coach is relatively easy to make. There are simple practices that can be adopted such as asking open questions and 'active listening' that can yield a lot of value. As managers in challenging environments we can forget that we are immersed in the present and consumed by tasks that need completing. The time to pause and reflect can disappear and therefore our opportunities to learn are diminished.

However, adopting simple changes in behaviour does not in itself result in a coaching *mindset*. Some extra value will be obtained, but ultimately there is a limit to what can be achieved by listening and questioning as a line manager.

Remember, the pure coach does not have direct responsibility for your own development; they merely help you identify the need for it.

As a coaching manager you must truly want to help people. Managers who see their staff as instruments for their own advancement will struggle with developmental coaching. They'll adopt some techniques that make them perform better in the long run than a directive manager, but the real power of coaching will not be realised.

Where some managers can go wrong is that they want to help staff, but their help actually constitutes advice and directive instruction.

Every time you use a directive approach towards your staff, you are inhibiting the opportunities for them to think for themselves and possibly solve the problem in the future, without bothering you!

Managers that adopt a coaching mindset tend to look

within themselves and use the coaching of others to increase not only the coachee's self awareness, but that of their own. They will serve their staff by genuinely supporting their development, and they will strive to be helpful rather than evaluative.

Along the way, a coaching manager will develop an individual coaching identity, that will be based upon their own personal values.

> **Reflection:** *In your current context, what will be possible as a result of you adopting a coaching mindset?*

The 'un-coach-ables'

There is one further difference between personal coaching and the practice of the coaching manager. Executives hire coaches out of choice. They are wanting help with something and the coach is brought in to assist.

Imagine the scenario where you are introduced to a coach upon the recommendation of your line manager. In fact, your line manager has read about the benefits of coaching and feels that you will be able to perform better after coaching.

How enthusiastic are you likely to feel about this?

This is an example that supports the perception that performance management is viewed as a remedial task, and that by association, coaching is similar as it is a method of improving an individual's performance. This is problematic for two reasons.

First, as we have discovered, coaching is related to learning. If the recipient doesn't want to learn, they are unlikely to embrace coaching. This might not be a conscious decision on the part of the individual; they may not be sufficiently self-aware to recognise that their actions are creating challenges for others.

Second, coaching is often deployed as means to 'fix' people. If there are specific weaknesses in an individual's performance, it could be that the individual may not also be receptive to coaching.

As a result, a considerable amount of time and effort is expended attempting to coach the 'un-coach-ables', rather than supporting able staff who are willing to grow.

Coaching should not be viewed as a panacea. The coaching manager will achieve far more by concentrating coaching upon receptive staff, so that their talents and abilities can be realised.

In the longer term, our fostering of a coaching culture will create an environment whereby those who have been coached will adopt the necessary mindset to coach others, resulting in a reduction of the impact of individual poor performance upon the performance of the collective.

Exercise

Reflect back over the conversations you have had over the past working week.

- What proportion of these discussions did you provide advice?
- What were your reasons for providing advice?
- What were your reasons for asking questions?

If your staff were less dependent upon your expertise,

RICHARD HILL, PhD

how would you spend your time?

6 DATA-DRIVEN

Being data-driven

More so than ever, the presence of data is a fundamental part of our working and personal lives. The consumption of data is also outstripped by the *production* of data; our continued engagement with mobile devices is creating data at an unprecedented rate.

As the capability of technology increases, and data becomes more widely available, it is possible to analyse and link data in new ways, finding answers to previously unanswered questions.

It is rational to conclude that if we can use data to improve our understanding of a given situation, then any subsequent decision that is taken will be superior to the historical situation, that had a heavier reliance upon instinct and subjectivity.

Certainly, it helps if the thinking prior to a decision can be audited in terms of the data that was used; our decisions should perhaps demonstrate provenance now.

Of course the situation is not quite as straightforward as it sounds, and there are many instances where data is used inappropriately or erroneously to draw conclusions that are just wrong.

As any scientist knows, the presentation of data can affect how it is received and acted upon, with disastrous consequences in some cases.

Universities are awash with data. In many cases, staff feel they are drowning in data. Student data, module data, quality reports, application data, programme health data, the list goes on.

A common challenge with university data is not its absence, but the recognition that it is frequently inaccessible.

Different systems, different formats, different assumptions, different reporting, all present barriers to the unification of data for universal decision making.

So what does it really mean to be data-driven?

The complexity of this situation will no doubt resonate with many HEI employees. But after a while, the perception that data is inaccessible can become a default assumption, even when it is not the case.

This feeds the attitude that 'shooting from the hip' or at best a 'heuristic approach' (if, indeed a method has been applied, though it is generally not the case) is an acceptable approach upon which to base important decisions.

Being data driven means that we expect to use data to enhance our systematic enquiry into current practices, so that we can inform a future course of action.

That insight may be articulated as a report of numbers, to initiate specific, directive instructions for corrective action. Or, it may be a rich source of qualitative feedback that can be used to shape conversations around enhancement.

> **Reflection:** *Think of an example where you have made a decision, but you would have preferred to have more data available. How might you prevent that situation from recurring?*

> **Reflection:** *Think of a situation where quantitative data was used as an attempt to explain a complex situation. What was the effect of this approach?*

Leading with data

One of the themes of this book is that of leadership. We can adopt certain behaviours to reinforce our underlying beliefs, and a coaching mindset is one part of that. We can set an example for our followers, by demonstrating that we live our values through our working practices. But how can we use data to lead?

One characteristic of leadership is about challenge. We can of course use data to challenge individuals, their beliefs and cultural norms. If we can trust the data, and the processes used to create it, then such data can be the basis of a convincing argument.

It can also be the basis of a culture of constraint, whereby individuals are reluctant to question, for fear of being 'shot-down' with numbers.

Creating a culture of challenge, without using data to suppress ideas and thinking, is in itself a challenge. Our leadership should be sufficiently supportive so that staff consume data critically, yet they will volunteer and explore the use of new and different data, if they feel that it enriches the enquiry.

A focus upon process is key here; leaders invest time in developing staff that understand what it means to systematically enquire, to be comfortable with inference and have the utmost confidence in the ability to assess the relative value and contribution of a data set.

This skill set is reinforced by leaders who use data to enhance and develop practice, rather than to diagnose and 'fix' weaknesses.

> ***Reflection:*** *The satisfaction of both students and staff is commonly reported for departments and HEIs as a whole. How does your institution use the data that is collected? What could be done to make better use of that data?*

Data for self-awareness

The act of collecting data about an organisational unit can be a powerful means of encouraging staff to reflect, which can be even more significant if the staff are involved in the data collection process themselves.

Increasing staff awareness of data that provides an assessment of their context drives distributed thinking about potential improvements.

Some issues will become immediately obvious, and not long after are resolved directly by staff without any intervention from management. Such an awareness improves an organisational unit's ability to understand itself, and as a consequence make decisions that are driven by the needs of the unit rather than the needs of an individual.

This approach also helps the unit towards a culture where individuals are trusted to investigate and act upon the issues that are important to the unit.

> **Reflection:** *Which dataset would be of greatest use to your team/department/organisation? How would it help them make better decisions?*

Exercise

There are two particular contexts for this exercise, either organisational or individual. Make a list of all of the information sources that you are aware of that relate to the object of your attention, whether it be an individual or the institution.

You will find it useful for later chapters if you record the exact location of the information, so that you can consult it later. Choose the context that is most applicable for your needs.

Organisational context

Look in the following places:

- Organisation intranet
    - Student performance
    - Programme/module health data
    - Application and enrolment data
    - Marketing information
    - Case study information

- Public websites

    - www.unistats.co.uk

    - University league tables

    - Organisational financial statements (it is also useful to look at competitor's financial statements as well).

- www.heidi.ac.uk - you may have to ask for an institutional account to use this service. Consult with your central administrative team.

- Quality Assurance Agency reports.

Individual context

If you are working with an individual (or upon yourself), then you will need to think about what sources of data are available. Some examples might be:

- Student feedback

- Timetabled teaching

- Research outputs

- Income generated

- External esteem

- Awards received

- 360 degree feedback

PART TWO

Part Two explains use of the **ADVANCE** model to support the development of a high performance culture.

7 ADVANCE OVERVIEW

ADVANCE was borne out of thousands of person-hours working on improvement projects, which varied from individuals developing themselves personally, through mentors and coaches facilitating the development of individuals, as well as senior leaders and managers who have teams, departments or institutions to transform in a positive way.

Improvement projects in the workplace can rapidly become complex, as the logic and rationality of systems and processes is called into question by the vagaries of human behaviour and interaction.

What might appear to be a relatively trivial task to reduce the lead-time of a process, will often mask a much richer, complicated set of human interactions between different stakeholders.

The more time we spend initiating and managing change, the more we realise that whilst 'the system' often receives the blame, it is how the staff interact with the system that causes the challenge.

When we are immersed in such complexity as leaders it can be challenging to retain both our own and our staff's focus. Larger organisations (especially universities) are practiced at finding work to do, as well as discovering project successes to report, irrespective of whether the original objective was achieved or not.

All too often it is the lack of a clearly articulated vision, that relates explicitly to the domain concerned, upon which suitable checks and balances can be made, that lets an improvement initiative wander off course.

What is needed is a model that supports the creation of a strategic view that is rooted in the correct environment, whilst also providing explicit links to tactical activities that are a priority for the change implementation.

The ADVANCE model illustrated in Figure 1, encapsulates the essential strategic and tactical prompts for the leadership of change initiatives. It is comprised of two stages.

The first stage is focused upon strategic thinking, and the components contained therein should be completed in order. This stage focuses on developing an in-depth, rich understanding of self awareness, and the environment in which the improvement will be instantiated, that will lead towards a concise, informed and aspirational vision statement.

This is followed by the tactical stage, which contains four key components to work with. There is no predetermined order to working with these principles, and the starting position will vary each time the ADVANCE model is applied.

However, each instantiation of ADVANCE will require

that all of the tactical aspects are called upon and addressed satisfactorily.

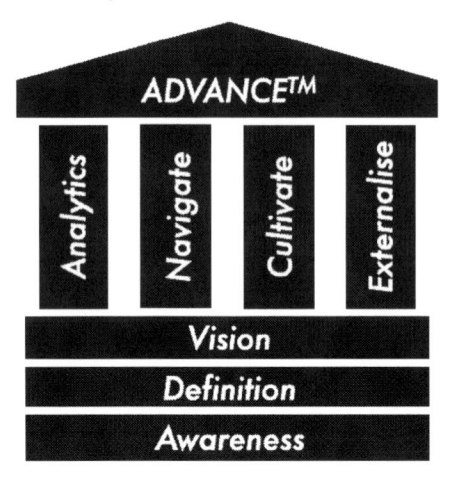

Fig. 1. The ADVANCE Model.

ADVANCE has been successfully used in a number of different ways, across a wide range of business domains. In the main though, ADVANCE is typically employed to lead and coach change in the following three situations:

- To take complete ownership of personal development. It is not uncommon for individuals to decide that there are aspects of their work or home life that they wish to improve. They make the conscious decision to lead their own development and use ADVANCE as the model.

- An alternative situation is an individual seeking out the support of an educational trainer or coach, to facilitate their own agenda of self improvement. In such cases. The coaching professional can use the ADVANCE model to help coachees construct their own personal development plan.

- The third scenario is that of working with groups of people. Increasingly, enterprises are seeking to empower their staff and develop leadership capacity. Managers in such environments find that they now have to lead change by describing a future, aspirational state, before they manage the requisite changes that make the necessary performance improvements. The problem domain may involve small teams, departments or even a whole institution, depending upon who owns and initiates the need for change. ADVANCE helps by ensuring that the essential strategic thinking occurs before moving onto tactical operations.

Reflection is an essential part of the ADVANCE model, and is crucial to its successful implementation, particularly when the tactical stage is invoked. Careful, regular and documented reflection ensures that progress is swift and benefits are realised at the earliest opportunity.

In particularly complex, bureaucratic environments, the reflection aspect of ADVANCE serves to expose unintended benefits that were hitherto obscured by cultural practices, tradition or convoluted systems of processes.

Why do we need another approach to leading change?

A lot of approaches and techniques for performance improvement, transformation or change management, include prescriptive tools and methods of working. Such approaches can work well when the specified tool is suited to its application (or more likely, the environment is sufficiently receptive of the tool).

It is likely that one or more elements of a tightly specified method may not be congruent with a particular domain, and there is a real risk that the whole improvement initiative is derailed. Experience tells us that most change initiatives have a relatively quiet audience that welcomes failure.

ADVANCE addresses this by specifying an overarching framework of essential activities and principles to work by. Each aspect of ADVANCE creates a checklist of characteristics to identify, specify, discover or facilitate, and it is through the cycle of reflection and evaluation that the leadership of change is adapted, refined and enhanced with respect to the entity that it has been applied to.

This enables ADVANCE to be tailored to its application domain, by including tools of choice, as the leader sees fit.

For instance, your experience of developing strategy might have included the classic internal/external analysis of Strengths, Weaknesses, Opportunities and Threats (SWOT).

ADVANCE specifies the outcomes from each stage – how you arrive at the outcome is left for you to specify – and this is one of the fundamental reasons why the applicability of ADVANCE to many different domains (including HE) has been successful.

Similarly, ADVANCE does not differentiate between the leadership of change as a personal activity upon the self, or as a development or coaching activity with a line manager or professional coach, nor does it cater only for the leadership of change across a department or institution.

ADVANCE is equally applicable across each of these scenarios, making it increasingly attractive for managers who have demands for leadership placed upon them and they recognise that the need for leadership is an opportunity for them to develop.

Such managers often find themselves wanting, with personal shortcomings that they feel the need to address.

They'll also have staff who will benefit from focused coaching, and may also have to turn the whole department around in terms of its overall performance. In such cases the single ADVANCE model can simultaneously serve a number of demands within one framework.

Another significant characteristic of ADVANCE is its ability to be used transparently within an established set of systems.

This is of particular use when the domain is complex, and where existing hierarchies and committee structures may already exist.

Monolithic institutions have great difficulty in changing such structures, and the organisational culture may demonstrate hostility towards changes to systems being initiated.

The strategy stage of ADVANCE ensures that not only is an accurate future state described, but that it fits within the existing culture, and that the leader of that change has sufficient self-awareness to see the change through to its conclusion.

This might require some interesting navigation around the current organisation such as committee structures, for instance, and the application of ADVANCE serves to identify and help evaluate both planned and emergent outcomes along the path of implementation.

Strategic phase

Figure 1 illustrates the ADVANCE Model. Organised in the illustration as a Greek temple, the strategic stage contains three foundation layers, without which the model cannot be constructed. These three layers are explored sequentially, from the ground up.

Awareness

The *Awareness* layer relates to the object of change. If you are applying ADVANCE to your own personal development, the object is you. If you are coaching a client with regard to their development needs, then the object of the focus is the client. If you have been given 12 months to turn a department/institution around, then the department or institution is clearly the object to be developed.

Definition

Building upon Awareness, we then construct a *Definition* of the environment in which the object of change resides. This could be an organisational context, or an external market, or the place that an individual finds themselves yearning to escape from. It is focused on discovering essential characteristics about the current environment, that will inform the eventual construction of a *Vision*.

Vision

The *Vision* comprises two elements. The first is a description of the future state that is aspired to. The second element identifies key indicators that will provide evidence of a successful change occurring.

This layer is typically the most concise of all – but it

needs careful preparation to be effective, as it is the story that you will need to tell time and time again, until you have achieved your aim.

If your aim is become less anxious about your administration duties, you will need to remind yourself of the sense of calm that you are working towards, and be able to say what the future will look and feel like.

If your department needs to become more agile, you will need to be able to not only visualise the enhanced way of working, but be able to relentlessly communicate it to those who will enact the change.

In all cases, the monitoring and reporting of improvement is a key component of success. You will need to see trends that are positive – or at least if they aren't, understand why – without having to cobble together different measures from disjointed data.

Tactical phase

Together, the three strategic, foundation layers prepare the ground for the erection of four tactical pillars: *Analytics, Navigate, Cultivate* and *Externalise*.

There is no prescribed order for tactics specified by ADVANCE. Each leader will implement tactics in different ways, some focusing on one or two principles, others choosing to tackle all four at once. Important principles to take note of are:

- For the tactical phase to work effectively, data is required from the *strategic* phase;

- While the starting point in the *tactical* phase is whatever seems appropriate, from experience it is useful to start with *Analytics* or *Navigate* as data (its discovery and consumption) is key to all stages and this is the most quantitative;

- By the time we are set to *Cultivate* a culture of positive transformation, it's much better to have the facts to hand. However, you may decide that the culture needs work before you collect data in earnest;

- When coaching individuals through ADVANCE, keeping to a sequence can help some clients who find it difficult to focus.

To summarise, ADVANCE is sufficiently flexible for you to develop your own approach, which may be different for each scenario that you apply it to. The *strategy* phase (*Awareness*, *Definition* and *Vision*) will give you the most accurate steer on which of the tactical components to commence with.

Analytics

The *Analytics* component relates to the specific data that is required, and the creation and maintenance of systems to enable its reporting. At its simplest level, it will report against the key indicators that are articulated in the *Vision*, themselves being related to the study of the environment from the *Definition* layer.

However, particularly when the object of change is a complex organisational entity, the overarching measures do not have any meaningful relation to the operational activities that take place.

For instance, how many of your staff read the financial statements of your institution?

How do you read and understand them?

How distant are the measures from the actual operations?

As such, the *Analytics* component creates a checklist of attributes and behaviours that will need to be in place to enable effective and meaningful reporting.

Navigate

Navigate helps make explicit the existing mechanisms of change and influence. Where do the power bases lie?

Which committee is the most effective?

Whose authority is required? Successful navigation of processes and systems can ensure the change initiatives achieve real progress. The *Navigate* component prompts us to check that the most effective route forward is plotted.

Cultivate

The *Cultivate* tactic is a reminder of the call to action to develop and grow. Real, lasting, embedded change can only be instigated into an environment that is engaged with the notion of growth.

You might be concentrating upon your own growth, the growth of others, or be you could be concerned with the scale or pace of growth required.

If you are responsible for a large operational function you may need work on propagating and delegating the responsibility of cultivation to others, to get the job completed in time.

Externalise

It is common for many of us to ignore any desire to *Externalise* any results. This might be because of modesty, indicative of a lack of self-confidence, or if you haven't had to do it before and you don't know where to start.

However, it is through constant communication of the desired outcome that we can hope to achieve success. A vital component is the function of externalising the success, and using this as a motivational tool to elicit more and accelerated achievement.

8 STRATEGY - AWARENESS

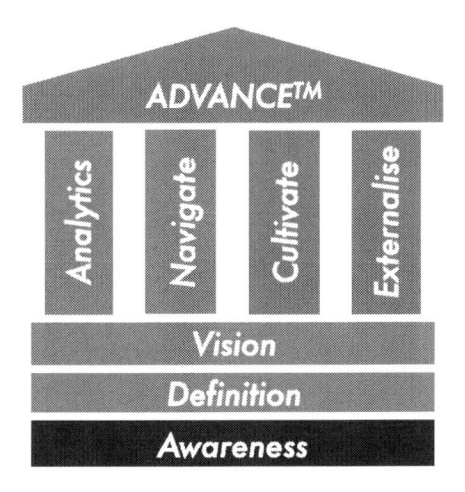

Awareness is a foundation stone of the ADVANCE model, upon which the rest of the 'temple' of activities is built. Its purpose is to establish the knowledge you possess of a situation, by increasing the consciousness of:

- Your self;

- Your surroundings.

Awareness constantly develops; the more you invest in your abilities to be responsive to your own or others' needs, the more you will discover to investigate.

This is an important component of the ADVANCE framework as it is all-too-common for potential agents of change to be distracted by myths, un-truths or misunderstanding. Know the facts before you embark upon change!

In common with all stages of ADVANCE, we shall collate some evidence upon which we can make decisions. MBA programmes the world over reinforce that before we can identify what needs to be done, we need to:

- Know your starting position (the 'as-is' situation);
- Understand what the destination looks like (the 'to-be' situation).

At this stage it doesn't matter whether the object of the transformation is yourself, an individual or a group of people; the key objective is to provide a critical awareness of the current situation.

However, the starting position for any leader (or potential leader) is to increase their own self-awareness, so it is logical to start by developing a personal reflection habit right away.

Before we embark upon a significant change initiative, it would perhaps appear sensible to realise that we should understand our own strengths and weaknesses.

Some appreciation of our own values and behaviours goes a long way towards maintaining peace of mind, and establishing a persona that is stable and respected by others.

Some simple questions we can ask of ourselves are likely to be as follows:

- What are we particularly effective at?

- What traits do we need to develop?

- Which activities do we need to draft-in help from others?

Our answers to such questions will help inform our self-perception. Of course, as we conduct our self analysis, we should be conscious of bias. In practice, either of the following situations may be evident:

- Our self-perception is inaccurate (we under or over-estimate our abilities), or;

- We don't feel as if we understand ourselves sufficiently. However, the external mandate is to conduct a successful personal/departmental/ organisational transformation, irrespective of how insecure we feel.

Inaccurate self-perceptions can tend to develop over time, if the focus of development activity is towards staff, rather than directed at yourself. For new line managers, the latter situation is most likely to strike a chord.

Whilst the *Awareness* stage is the first step of the approach, it is clear that if you are faced with a burgeoning mandate to get going and implement change, you will not have much time to perform a deep analysis of yourself.

This shouldn't be regarded as a major barrier to success though.

It is inevitable that the experience of transforming the performance of an academic department will result in significant personal changes. You will be different as a result.

What is important, is to establish some basic mechanisms that will quickly report upon the characteristics that are important to you. These simple reports will assist your own self-monitoring and enable you to identify strategies that work (for you) in your particular context.

Perhaps the most challenging scenario is where an individual has an inaccurate perception of themselves, that has developed over a number of years of hard-gained 'experience'.

In such cases the initial self-appraisal might need to be supplemented by external help, for instance by consulting close colleagues, friends, a mentor, or even a personal coach, in order to achieve an objective view.

The assumption here is that you either have an accurate perspective upon your own abilities, or that you are sufficiently interested and motivated to obtain that understanding.

This won't necessarily prevent you from encountering staff whose self-perception is misaligned with their behaviour, but at least you will begin to appreciate some of the challenges that this situation can present, when faced with the prospect of managing such people through a period of substantial change.

The coaching manager recognises the importance of self-awareness. We can learn a lot about others when we know how to make sense of our own behaviours.

Understanding our own behaviours, and our responses to various stimuli comes from a deep, critical analysis of how we operate on a daily basis.

How do we obtain this insight?

Reflection as a habit

An extremely effective method for improving awareness is to engage in reflective practice. As managers working in intense environments, we acquire experience and use that as our own evidence base with which to compare and contrast future situations.

Reflection is a practice that is most powerful when it becomes a habit. Often, even as critical people, we shall hit upon something and think *"what a good idea! I'll start doing that right away!"*.

We'll rush into the new behaviour with vigorous enthusiasm, and we may even see some benefits appear quickly. But what happens next? Often, we're not sure. What we do know is that we might become a bit less diligent, and we might cut a few corners.

We shall justify to ourselves that we are still enjoying the benefits of our new behaviour, even if we don't follow it to the letter. After all, we should be able to tailor the new way of working to suit our individual needs, shouldn't we?

If we are honest, after a short while the enthusiasm subsides. We stop practicing the new behaviour (that we originally recognised as a 'good idea') and we revert back to how we were beforehand. Even though we might have witnessed some tangible benefits.

Personal organisation is a good example of this. How

often do people fall off the wagon of enhanced productivity?

How many systems/pens/notebooks/planners/index cards and binder clips are purchased during the initial rush of excitement?

We know that personal productivity is usually improved when we write things down, and organise those things logically. We also know that the key to retaining the productivity is regular maintenance – if the system gets into a mess, the organisation goes out of the window, and takes the productivity with it.

Reflection is no different. It needs to be performed regularly and thoughtfully, and it needs to be recorded to obtain the maximum impact from your time.

The reflection challenge

Whilst our desire to become more leaderly is a compelling argument to engage in some transformation, there is a practical limit as to how forensic you can be about recording things.

Over the years I have tried all sorts of approaches, and in the main, I've wasted an inordinate amount of time trying to implement systems for reflection that have been far too complicated. The net result of this has been a long-term frustration with 'systems', and at times a disillusionment with the whole reflective process.

Fortunately, I've witnessed sufficient successes as a direct result of reflection, that has kept me searching for 'a better way'. After persevering for many years I've found my system – and even though it works for me, I've also seen it work for the many of people that I've taught, mentored and coached as well.

Like all habits that we keep, the basis of my reflection workflow is simplicity. If it's inconvenient or too time consuming to maintain, then it won't stick. I need to be able to extract sufficient value out of the process to keep me motivated, otherwise, there is no point in continuing.

Collect

The principle behaviour that needs to be fully embedded is that of collection. To reflect critically you need accurate facts to draw upon.

This means that events in our lives need to be written down before they are coloured by our feelings, emotions, recollections and all of the other biases that our characters introduce into the mix. I do this daily, and it doesn't take as long as you might think.

In the early days I attempted to write daily because it seemed to be the logical thing to do. A working day is a reasonable chunk of time to reflect upon, and quite a lot can happen if the day is eventful.

In fact it was far too ambitious. Why?

Because I was writing down too much detail. I was collecting too much information. The burden of writing 500 words every day became too great, so I fell off the wagon.

Now I don't worry about word count. I don't sit and become anxious if I can't find anything to write. I have one simple rule:

RICHARD HILL, PhD

Every workday I will write for a minimum of 10 minutes before I read my email.

I've arrived at 10 minutes through trial and error. You might find that 5 minutes is sufficient, or that you need at least 15 minutes. That is up to you. In terms of getting the habit embedded into your daily life, I would tend to suggest starting small and working upwards to a block of time that you can regularly maintain.

Some days the 10 minutes is meaningless, as I am still writing 40 minutes later! Conversely, there are days when I don't reach 10 minutes either. But I do write every day.

There are, of course days when it's a struggle to get started. It was a major stumbling block for me until I was given this tip from an experienced author:

"If you don't have anything to write, write THAT down, repeatedly. You'll soon have something to say."

So, when inspiration seems elusive, I write: *I have nothing to write this morning. I have nothing to write this morning. I have nothing to write ...*

Rest assured, a topic makes itself available quite quickly.

A frequent question I receive from aspiring reflective leaders, relates to *how* they should write their reflections; *"what style should I use?"* is quite common. I have found that subconsciously, people write for an audience other than themselves.

They want to make sure that what they write is grammatically correct, free of spelling errors, and relatively polished in terms of structure, just like we were taught at school. They often look surprised when I tell them to *"write for yourself"*.

What I actually mean is that their writing should be for their own consumption. It is not meant to be public. So don't worry about mistakes, as long as the event/message is recorded. Stern schoolteachers have a lot to answer for when it comes to suppressing creative and free expression through writing.

Try writing without constraints; don't worry about capitalisation, grammar and punctuation. Don't re-write, and concentrate on getting the thoughts out of your head. Forget editing and correction, just collect. Try it, and feel the liberation.

Another question is *where* I should write. Generally, most people can identify a location to do it, one that is quiet and free from distraction. If you work in a communal office, headphones are useful.

However, most enquirers are more concerned with the location of the actual words – all those thoughts that are now recorded, are out of their heads. There is, of course a concern that somebody else might read them.

Notebooks are great for capture. You don't need to plug them in, or wait for them to boot up. But they can be misplaced, and they are easy to read which may be a problem if you're nervous about your thoughts being made public.

I do use a notebook – a tiny one that goes almost everywhere with me – but I tend to use it more for recording ideas than actually reflecting. In terms of my daily-before-email capture, I prefer to use technology to assist.

In the same way that you can indulge in stationery, there is a multitude of private journaling software, that has features over and above what you would might expect in a normal word processor.

Keeping with my premise of simplicity, I don't bother with any of those. I've found what works for me, and I can do it with freely available tools.

Reflect

Once you have a secure container, into which you regularly place your thoughts, you can now start to prepare for subsequent stages in the reflection workflow. The data that you have captured should be raw, factual and to the point. Some days you'll list bullet points.

Other times you'll write an essay. This information will be rich with detail, and when you start to look back at what you have recorded, you will almost certainly identify themes that are evident in your behaviour.

This stage by itself can be transformational; I have discussed this with reflection converts in the past, and they feel that they derive significant benefit from the regular act of collecting and then just reviewing what they have gathered.

However, whilst the collection habit is a major development point, there is much more to come yet. I tend to spend 10 minutes per week reviewing what I have written over the previous five days, and during this process I identify and select developmental themes to pursue.

More often than not these themes are self-evident within the first two minutes of the review, but some of the more transformational items may take longer to surface.

So, the act of reviewing is a crucial activity to maximise the benefit of daily writing.

How often should we review? Again, this can depend upon the level of activity that you experience during a typical workday. In the cut and thrust of a project that is behind schedule, there may be more events to review, but less time to do it.

In quieter periods there will ample time for review, but perhaps less activity to record. I suggest weekly reviews at first, at least until you get the behaviours embedded as part of your daily routine.

The output of the review process should be a written reflection. What is important here is that the review is a piece of writing that is solely based upon a) what you have recorded during the week, and b) your thoughts as they have developed over the five days.

At first you may find this challenging, as there is a natural tendency to reflect upon everything that you can remember, which might include events and thoughts that you haven't recorded.

If you get into the habit of including ad hoc topics during the review process, then you will undermine the value of daily recording.

One approach to improve the value of your review is to use some simple prompt questions, that can become a lightweight review template as follows:

- *"What went well?"*

- *"What didn't go so well?"*

- *"Would I do it again?"*

In time, and with practice, you'll become more accurate and create more comprehensive daily reflections. This will help reinforce the habit by improving the value that you extract from the process.

Now this doesn't mean that you should dismiss any thoughts or recollections that the review process may trigger. Just write them down separately, so that they are available for consideration during the next review.

Project forwards

As you build your base of evidence through reflection, not only will you recognise patterns in your behaviour, but you will be better placed to experiment with different ways of working.

In Chapter 4 we looked at using a simple change in question technique to start embedding coaching practice into our daily conversations. Add to this a simple reflection workflow and you'll be able to gather evidence in relation to the results.

As a busy leader you may be asking *"so what?"*. (As an aside, this is an excellent question that should find its way into our thinking more. Beware of saying it aloud though, as those in earshot can find it a little wearing if it is used too frequently.)

As you build your evidence, your self-awareness will increase. You'll begin to spot areas of weakness that need development, and you'll have the habits in place to investigate them by experimentation, followed by your evaluation of the results.

Soon you will be able to *project* forward your ideas for

development and growth, and then proactively plan activities to reflect upon.

If you are using the two prompt review questions from above as a template, you could add one further question:

- *"How would I approach this situation in the future?"*

Let's say that you find networking at conferences makes you feel uncomfortable. Through reflection you identify that it's the conversation after the introductory small-talk that you find challenging.

After further thought you come up with a few ideas to try out. But rather than wait for the next conference, you decide to use a local event where you can experiment and then quickly retire if it doesn't go to plan (it probably won't be that catastrophic).

The act of planning to develop yourself by projecting forward means that you are taking the initiative with respect to your development as a leader.

This example illustrates how we can plan our future activities, to gain specific experience that we are seeking for our own development. This could also apply to the selection of processes as well.

For instance, managers can find their roles make them isolated - there are not that many peers to talk to - and development discussions may be too infrequent, if they occur at all.

This could highlight a need to gather data about an individual's behaviour; the 'blind side' of our personality, that everyone else sees except ourselves.

A common tool for this is a 360 degree review, where

subordinates, peers and line managers complete a set of questions that prompt them to reflect about you in the workplace.

When managers consciously reflect upon their own behaviour in a regular and structured way, they often report a feeling of being compelled to understand themselves to a greater depth.

Now, just imagine what your department would achieve if a few of your staff could acquire the reflection habit?

Organisational reflection

I would always recommend that managers adopt their own reflection routine as a priority, since there is so much to be gained from the habit.

But the act of understanding what it means to reflect about ourselves makes it more straightforward to both support those that we coach as they commence a journey of greater awareness, as well as simplifying how we apply reflection to a third party.

Of course by 'third party' I am referring to how we can govern the reflection of an organisational unit such as a department or even the whole institution.

Reflecting upon the actions and behaviours of an organisation is a useful practice as it helps us to become more critical appraisers of the systems and cultures that exist.

As we discover through personal reflective activity, we are driven to acquire more data about ourselves. This is no different for the organisational unit.

But once we exhaust all the usual sources of data, we often find that we want to build an even richer picture by finding new sources of data that we would not have considered before, or at least if we knew of their existence we wouldn't normally have sufficient motivation to access them.

Systematic reflection about our existing context can provide the motivation to delve deeper, beyond the myths and organisational chatter, to construct a more accurate representation that is based on data we have acquired.

In the same way that we might visit a Doctor for a health check, we can look at the 'vital signs' of an institution and construct a perspective from the data.

Here are some typical sources of data that are available for an institution:

- Student performance;

- Lecturer performance (www.ratemylecturer.com can be an interesting read);

- Programme/module health data;

- Application and enrolment data;

- Marketing information;

- Self-evaluation documentation;

- Case study information.

Example - department profile

By way of an example, we shall look at one common scenario for academic management: how to profile the staff in an academic department. We shall explore the use of some straightforward analysis to ascertain the generic capability mix of a body of academic staff.

Before we can think of what transformation is possible with a department, it is imperative that we understand what our staff base is capable of. To reach this perspective we need to be able to:

1. Identify what the fundamental characteristics of an academic are;

2. Describe the individual profiles of staff in relation to fundamental characteristics;

3. Represent the strengths and weaknesses presented by the existing staff base;

4. Identify any immediate areas for staff development.

For each of the items 1-4 above, it is useful to have a point of reference in terms of an ideal 'staff profile'. Each academic manager will have their own perspective as to what constitutes the 'ideal', and this will have been shaped by values, beliefs and prior experience in academia.

If you have come from outside of academia into a management position, then your perspective is likely to be distinct from the academic 'norm'. However, this may have been the intention of those who recruited you!

What follows is a description of an academic profile that can suit many institutions, and indeed has been used as the basis of many successful transformations. We refer to this model profile as the *Holistic Academic*.

The Holistic Academic (HA) is characterised by three fundamental components:

- Teaching quality. The HA engages learners in such a way that their experience is transformative. Learners achieve their potential and practice the processes of research. The HA systematically evaluates their own teaching practice and strives for its continual enhancement.

- Research quality. The processes of research are utilised to create new knowledge that is disseminated through peer-reviewed processes. The product of these processes is recognised leadership within a research community that establishes an external reputation for the individual.

- Income generation. The HA can apply knowledge to real-world challenges, to create social or economic impact that is validated by external funding sources.

Whilst there are three components, it is not necessarily assumed that each characteristic receives 33% of the HA's time. Some academics will allocate more time to teaching, others will dedicate time to income generation.

Once the conceptual model of an academic has been adopted, it is relatively easy to 'profile' individuals by the amount of time they spend in each area. Please note that the use of time as a 'currency' is deliberate. Within many HEIs, the systems for 'academic work planning' use time allowances to represent contributions to different activities.

If you are work-planned to 550 contact hours per year, you would allocate approximately 180 hours to each category perhaps.

You may plan workloads to another figure such as 1600 for instance. This doesn't matter, you just alter the proportions to suit your situation.

The next stage is to compile a staff profile summary that shows how much time each member of staff has allocated to each one of the three categories identified above.

Think of this as a quick check – don't get too bogged down in the detail. Let's have a look at an example:

Staff	Teaching	Research	Income	Total
W. D.	180	190	180	550
U. J.	360	40	150	550
S. M.	400	40	110	550
J. F.	550	0	0	550
K. P.	500	0	50	550
S. J.	450	0	100	550
Totals:	2440	270	590	3300

Table 1. Academic staff workload allocation by Teaching, Research and Income Generation.

If we consider Table 1, we can observe the following:

- W. D. has the most balanced allocation of the

group.

- J. F. only engages with teaching activity.

- Three academics engage in research and income generation.

- Only one academic does not engage in income generation.

- All academics teach.

- 74% of the available capacity is allocated to teaching (2440/3300).

- 18% of the capacity is allocated to income generation (590/3300).

- 8% of the capacity is allocated to research (270/3300).

Reflection: *What questions might this pose for the academic manager?*

Once there is a clearer picture about the allocation of academic time (a relatively expensive resource), it often follows that the value derived from that investment is then queried.

For instance, if 18% of the pay budget is being allocated to income generation, how much income was actually received?

Of course, these arguments are rarely one dimensional. An academic manager may decide to invest academic resource over a longer period, to achieve much greater income streams.

They may also recognise that the processes of staff engaging with external partners has intangible side-effects such as increased visibility within the region for the HEI, the formation of stronger social networks, or more industrial partners with which to bid for research grants.

The coaching manager might then investigate a little deeper. How much of the research activity is published in 2 star journals?

However, the interesting thing here is that such strategic decisions are more effective when they are informed by data, and the accumulation of such data is relatively easy to come by.

This simple profiling exercise increases your awareness of what is possible right now, as well as indicating what you might consider for the future.

The next step is to perform a simple analysis of the academic unit by noting any particular strengths and weaknesses that arise out of the workload planning data:

- Strengths
  - Good teaching capability;
  - Significant income generation capacity (most academics);
  - Evidence of one HA;
  - Can subsidise loss of student fees with income generation;
- Weaknesses

- Minimal contribution to a research culture;

- Staff profiles imbalanced;

- Potential lack of external reputation/branding.

The analysis paints an interesting picture. Based upon what we see right now, there is a clear emphasis towards teaching, and to a lesser extent income generation.

This might suggest that there is plenty of teaching capacity, with perhaps a good student experience if that is the apparent focus of the department (or indeed this may not be the case).

There is also one example of a HA, so in this particular environment it is possible to aspire to a more balanced workload.

Finally, the significant capacity for income generation suggests that it might be relatively easy to use this capability to shore up any future shortfall in student numbers as a result of market volatility.

But what about the weaknesses?

The small amount of research activity indicates that there is a potential opportunity to build a brand through academic esteem and reputation. So maybe this is an area that is ripe for development.

The opportunities presented by a shift towards research activity may be more pervasive and beneficial in the wider sense, or indeed they may be too risky for the HEI to undertake.

At this point, we have already deepened our understanding of the academic staff base. We can use a model profile to identify where the staff capabilities lie, and thus we are then able to generate a profile for the academic unit as a whole.

A rudimentary analysis then assists the identification of key questions that we can pose and subsequently answer, with more data.

One advantage of this approach is that it scales easily. You can profile a subject area, a school, a department, a faculty or even an institution.

All you need to know is the hours allocated to each of the three categories for each member of staff, and how to access the data from the institution's work planning system.

If the system is common, then an automated report can be created by the HEI's central information systems function, and this can be used as a part of an analytics tool to monitor shifts in work practices as part of your transformation initiative.

Exercise

In order to develop your self awareness you will need to establish a reflection habit. Frequent, written reflection will build you a base of data upon which you can ask questions and draw conclusions about yourself. Follow the four steps below to get things underway:

Step 1. Commit to writing for 10 minutes per day
Step 2. Once a week, read through what you have written during the week. Write down any observations.

Step 3. As you begin to observe patterns, plan small changes to your behaviour, the results of which will be recorded in your daily reflection.

Step 4. Reflect upon the results, produce new plans, and continue.

If you are interested in improving the performance of an organisational unit, you will need to gather data about that unit.

You will probably find a lot of data within your local intranet, but failing that you should make acquaintances with central staff in the following functions: strategic planning, quality, learning and teaching support, admissions, marketing and finance.

Be open with them when they ask what you want the information for. I have found that most people are genuinely interested in helping. Some examples of potential data of interest are:

- Student applications, enrolments, retention, tariffs on entry, graduate destinations;

- Student feedback surveys;

- Student performance, achievement, demographic;

- Teaching and learning measures;

- Curriculum assessment, portfolio 'health', External Examiner's reports and responses;

- Staff workloads, staff absence;

- Staff qualifications;

- Outcomes from committee meetings;

- Financial indicators, income profile, research income, third-stream income, Staff/Student ratio.

At this stage it is probably sufficient to start the process of collating data together with the associated reports that are generated for management purposes.

Your initial investigation will itself be an education, as you discover not only what data is produced, but who produces it and for what reason.

When you come across an area that is of interest, do some simple analysis as per the 'department profile' example.

Remember to keep the analysis simple, and where possible define a 'model concept' against which you can make comparisons.

In the case of the staff profiling example, the model concept is the *Holistic Academic* (I'm still attempting to recruit one).

You will also uncover reports and data that is produced as a matter of course, where the real purpose of the report has been forgotten.

However, these reports can help directly by providing the data you need, or indirectly by informing your view of the character of the institution.

Don't underestimate the effect of conversation that is stimulated by your enquiry. Staff will relay the 'organisational memory' to you through various stories, which will enhance your awareness of what change is

THE ACADEMIC COACH

possible (as well as providing some entertainment).

9 STRATEGY - DEFINITION

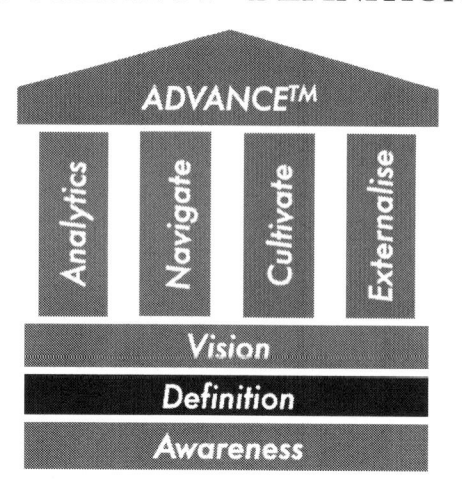

If you have completed the exercise from Chapter 8 you will have a much more informed picture of your surroundings. The *Definition* stage follows on from the data you have gathered during the *Awareness* stage.

You are beginning to understand what you/client/department/organisation is capable of, and now you need to define that in the context of the environment.

The environment may be local as in your immediate surroundings. Conversely, it may be a national or global domain. Once the data is consolidated, you can start to ask questions about the data, to explore potential scenarios. Relevant questions at this stage might include:

- How is success measured in the domain?
- What policy changes may affect future trends?
- When will the management structure be changed?
- How will a merger of subjects take place?
- What challenges are there for the working culture?
- How much time and energy am I able to invest?

What we are attempting to do is to a) cross-validate the various data sources, b) identify any omissions in data, c) look for areas of development potential, and d) define a position in relation to the external environment.

Essentially this is all about defining and qualifying the important facts; what data will you use, the data you are likely to need, and what data you currently have.

External data

Data from the *Awareness* component is concentrated on *internal* sources. It is the detail that permits us to be introspective and deep in our reflection and subsequent analysis.

Having acquired that data, we are now consulting

external data sources. We do this for two reasons.

First, it helps qualify the internal stories the institution tells itself. These stories may be more or less authentic. For example, a department may have the perception that it delivers teaching of 'high quality'.

It is therefore important to understand what data supports this assertion in terms of quantitative assessment and qualitative reports.

However, once the external data is scrutinised, the internal data will be placed into a context that includes data from other HEIs. What might be considered excellent internally may only be average for the sector.

It is amazing how staff can sometimes believe the stories that arise from daily conversation; such stories become accepted fact when they are left unchallenged.

Second, when we consult external data sources we can understand the position that the subject area/department/institution occupies in the sector at large. This helps build a more accurate picture of identity, and can both shatter illusions and signal potential for the future.

Most HEIs identify a 'benchmark group' of competitors, that describes other HEIs that are thought to be competing for the same students, or similar research income.

During your investigation you can scrutinise the list of HEIs in your own benchmark group and ascertain what position in the sector they occupy. If you are concerned with a subject area, you could look at that as well.

There is normally a difference between the institutional

position and that of a subject area; this of course makes sense as the institution is an aggregation of all of the subjects it offers.

However, you might observe some potential tensions for certain activities, particularly around teaching and research. A university with a favourable reputation for teaching quality may contrast with a department that demonstrates excellence in its subject discipline research.

This insight will help shape your eventual approach to transformation.

Fortunately, external data is generally easily accessible using the internet. One advantage of public data is that it allows us to look at competitor institutions, and then make informed comparisons. These are some data sources that are publicly available:

- Public websites

    - UNISTATS - www.unistats.co.uk;

    - University league tables (various);

    - Organisational financial statements;

    - www.heidi.ac.uk - you may have to ask for an institutional account to use this service. Consult with your central administrative team;

- Quality Assurance Agency reports - http://www.qaa.ac.uk/en

A large part of this effort is organisation. You are collating data from myriad systems, which are disparate and separate. You are identifying links between the data that will provide you with a comprehensive understanding of the object in question.

All of this requires systematic enquiry, patience and diligence to build the most accurate view possible. Effort expended here will substantially increase your confidence in the foundations of your eventual vision.

Exercise

We shall now augment the internal data that was collated during *Awareness* with external data.

Step 1. Identify external data sources.

Step 2. Identify a benchmark comparison group that is relevant to your investigation.

Step 3. Collate the data.

Step 4. Identify specific areas of interest and apply some simple analysis. For example, for a given benchmark of HEIs, compare the proportions of income generated through tuition fees, funding councils and 'other'.

Step 5. Use the external data to assist the validation of internal data (both quantitative and qualitative). Some examples could include:

- External Examiner reports against Quality committee minutes, module action plans and QAA audit data;

- Published student/staff ratios (SSR) against academic workload plans, timetable information and module description documents;

THE ACADEMIC COACH

- Student surveys against module feedback and staff/student committee meetings;

- Departmental enhancement plans with programme/course enhancement plans.

10 STRATEGY - VISION

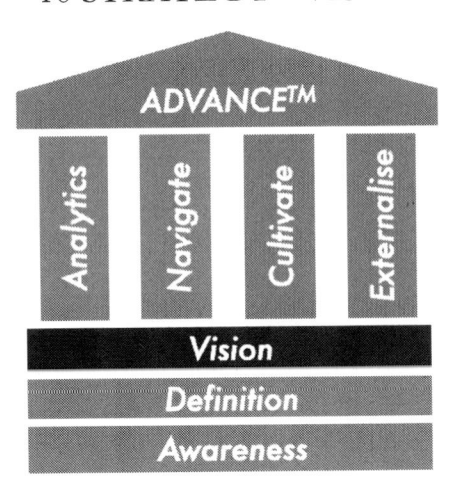

Vision is the culmination of the strategic phase of ADVANCE. It's about looking to the future, a time where success has been achieved, and then translating this into a story that people can relate to.

The *Vision* helps us relate the here and now, with all its messiness and complexity, to the future, aspirational state.

It makes explicit the measures that will hold us accountable for our actions, with the comfort that these measures will help drive the transformation forward.

Leadership development texts often refer to the importance of vision – having a vision, constructing a vision and the communication of the vision. But what is a vision, and how important is it to have one?

A vision is some description of a future state. In terms of planning for development, it is anticipated that the vision will be aspirational. Aspirational enough to stretch the object being developed, without demoralising if the aspiration is too ambitious.

Successful communication of the vision is of utmost importance. Many a realistic vision has been left stranded by poor communication – the enablers of the vision, those who will follow your 'North Star', either misunderstood the message, or just *"didn't get it"*.

This can be disastrous and is a scenario we shall work on systematically to avoid. If your vision is clear, and repeated often, the work to be done will follow logically and performance improvements will be witnessed.

So where do we start?

If a critical success factor of a vision is how it is communicated, then we need to ensure that:

- The recipients understand and can visualise the future state that you are describing. This means that it needs to be described using their language – the language of the industry they work in, using day-to-day expressions and statements particular to the domain;

- There are obvious and explicit items to measure progress against. Everybody likes to see progress, and when we are in the thick of it, we can sometimes lose sight of the overall goals. A clear vision identifies the 'big picture' in terms of key measures, and serves to remind us of the importance of persisting to realise the vision rather than getting caught-up in the daily complexity of life.

The importance of communicating a vision is fundamental to the effective delegation of objectives to staff. If they interpret a different vision, you'll get a sustained effort that works against you. Vision creation can be a powerful force.

> **Reflection:** *When was the last time (if ever) that you sat down and described what you wanted from your professional life? Your personal life? Both?*

To ensure that a vision is relevant to your domain, then you will need to consider:

- Your external working environment. What measures are the standard for the industry? What are the benchmarks that you will be exceeding?

- Your internal environment. How aligned are you with the internal processes/culture? Where does the agency for successful change lie within the institution?

Successful completion of the *Definition* component highlights data that is missing and prompts additional activity to fill the gap. Thus ADVANCE is rarely treated as a linear process in which we pass through each stage once only. Rather it should be seen as a model that prompts refinement and iteration.

If some information is lacking from the vision, we need to return to the *Definition* component. Inevitably, some aspects will reveal insight that may improve the definition of another component. This is to be expected, embraced and ultimately, exploited for maximum benefit.

Aspirational, but realistic

This is a common concern, especially if you have little or no prior experience of vision construction. It is important to rely on the data you have collected. The fact that you have done this as part of *Definition* will substantially increase your chances of success.

Why quote a 20% increase in applications when the market median is 12%?

Such a statement may be too aspirational. Conversely, a 5% increase might be judged as too conservative, or too risk-averse. This will propagate silent messages that will sabotage your vision from the outset – people want to be led, not constrained.

You should also consider the number of items that you will need to describe your future state. It is surprising how many of my coachees dive in and create a list of a dozen or so items to measure.

This is symptomatic of a directive management mindset, and needs to be reconsidered when approaching the construction of a vision. My question to them is simple:

"What success is your market leader known for?"

After some initial, irrelevant detail, it quickly becomes

apparent that there is a much shorter list of items that are important. This list might have between 3-5 crucial measures, that really make the market leader stay out in front of the rest.

> **Reflection:** *Which institution/department would you regard as a market leader? What are your reasons for this judgement?*

From your earlier data gathering work, you will have no doubt read the vision statements of other universities. Whilst there will be differences, you will have seen a lot of similarity.

And so, you might say, what is the point of a vision that is common across most of the sector, if not across industry as a whole?

After all, don't we all want to "offer the best student employment opportunities" and "attract world-class academic staff"?

Of course we do. But the realisation of this vision is specific to an organisation, and therefore the operational objectives that achieve the vision will vary from university to university.

A vision needs to be sufficiently abstract and concise to enable it to be repeated until it is completely embedded within the organisation, so that it can be recalled and referred to during daily work.

Therefore, the vision should be seen as much more than just a brief articulation of a future state. It needs substantiating with a set of objectives that can be measured.

These two components – the future state, together with

the list of objectives in a narrative – make up the output of the *Vision* component of ADVANCE.

Getting started

Unless you have been thinking and talking about it for some time, the construction of a vision tends to be mostly a cyclical process. We need to understand our desire for aspiration if we are to specify sufficiently stretching objectives.

We need to understand the measures if our vision is to be realistic.

During many workshops I have witnessed a combination of approaches to vision construction. Some senior managers make bold statements in relation to a burning issue for their organisation, and this becomes the focal point. Relevant measures in the industry drive the construction of the Vision statement.

Other situations (typically in public sector and educational leadership settings) bring forth aspirational statements that require subsequent translation into measures that are relevant to the sector.

One example is that of 'reputation'. *"How can my educational institution improve its research reputation?"*

Another way of thinking about a vision is to imagine how the objectives will actually be realised through management activities. Some leaders ignore this, maintaining a clear separation between the leadership and management concepts, concentrating on the 'what' and 'why', rather than the 'how' and 'who'.

However, leaders that consider how their managers will

delegate, can also gain some insight into the culture of their organisation.

A by-product of vision construction is the realisation that an organisation is too heavily micro-managed, and that traits of leadership such as autonomy and empowerment, need more emphasis during the working day.

This has substantial implications for the organisation as a whole, and may, in fact warrant a clear steer from the vision statement and objectives that a culture change is required and has to happen.

Of course, this can be challenging to measure, but itself is an example of how a vision can actually become specific to its target environment.

Such a public declaration of the need to change fundamentally can also be a powerful statement that important issues will be tackled head-on. This helps those who require reassurance whilst realising the vision, as well as clearly identifying those staff who are likely to experience difficulties fitting into the future state.

Process-led vision creation

One situation that HEI managers can find themselves in the middle of, is having the responsibility to transform the performance of an academic unit within an institution.

This requires some appreciation that an overall institutional vision will exist, and therefore if you are to use a more tailored, local vision to help lead the necessary adjustments, it is important that explicit linkages are visible between the two vision statements.

However, if your current institutional vision is not clear, or it is undergoing consultation and review, then you may need to prepare for more than one potential vision for your department.

For instance, your institution might have signified that it wishes to 'change mission' in order to become financially stable.

This might be achieved by an outlook that is more enterprising; however, a HEI, or a department within an institution can be enterprising in many different ways, from adopting a more commercial approach to direct engagement with the business community, through to the expansion of the teaching business into new markets (international, franchising, e-learning, etc.).

The process of gathering data and performing some basic analysis as described in the *Definition* component will no doubt have strengthened the perspective you hold in relation to what potential can be achieved.

But it's also important to remember that your colleagues will probably not have completed the same exercise, and in many cases they will have no interest in doing so.

One way to address this is by involving staff in the process of using data as early as possible, with a view to building a culture that naturally produces and consumes data for the purposes of continuous improvement.

As a leader you need to translate the aims of the institution into operational plans, and in doing so describe work that is meaningful to the recipient. They need to understand what is required, if the vision is to be realised.

In such circumstances, vision creation requires a process that should be focused upon the development of academic staff. It should be designed to align operational activities to strategic objectives, by making clear, negotiated declarations of what is to be achieved over a given period, and then taking an evidence based approach to evaluate the results.

Briefly, the key principles are that the process is:

- Focused upon development;
- Outcomes are negotiated and agreed at the outset;
- Individuals are held to account;
- Judgements are based on evidence.

The first step is to understand what operational targets are relevant for your vision.

Declaring the targets

At this point, let's assume that there is a vision in place. There needs to be some aspirational, future state that you can link operational targets to. This will provide the 'story' that staff can relate to, and as a result be able to identify their developmental needs.

To help describe this process, we shall make use of an example. You may choose to keep a pen and some paper to hand, to make notes as you go along. This will make it much easier when you repeat the exercise with your own data.

We are going to start with the vision statement and measures profile:

THE ACADEMIC COACH

"The department will have an international reputation for the high-quality provision of teaching and research, to prepare graduates for professional careers.

It will attract highly qualified academic staff with international esteem, and be recognised as a leading contributor to educational, research and industrial partnerships.

Significant social and economic impact will be delivered by cultivating industrial projects to sustain a diverse set of income streams.

The vision will be achieved by:

- *Delivering a high-quality portfolio that is relevant to the needs of industry;*

- *Creating a student experience that beats the sector median;*

- *Developing peer credibility amongst academic staff by increasing external activities;*

- *Creating and disseminating knowledge for social and economic benefit, both regionally and nationally."*

Measures profile:

Performance Indicator	Present	5 years from now
Income	90% Teaching 8% Research 2% Other	78% Teaching 10% Research 12% Other
Graduate employability	65%	85%
Student satisfaction	Bottom quartile (25th percentile)	> Median (50th percentile or above)

From the brief details above, there are some clear targets for the department to achieve, which are described as part of the 'measures profile'. These are operational targets which are measurable, and have a timeline in which they are to be achieved (5 years).

But what about the text of the vision statement? Some interesting phrases include:

- *"international reputation for the high-quality provision of teaching and research";*

- *"to prepare graduates for professional careers";*

- *"attract highly qualified academic staff with international esteem";*

- *"recognised as a leading contributor to educational, research and industrial partnerships";*

- *"significant social and economic impact"*;

- *"cultivating industrial projects"*;

- *"sustain a diverse set of income streams"*.

For a moment, think ahead to the future. You have successfully achieved the required transformation, by proactively managing the performance of your staff.

How will you evidence the achievements, beyond the simple measures of income profile, NSS and league table position?

What evidence would satisfy you of someone's claim that they had established an international reputation in teaching?

You might be interested in the amount of funded pedagogic research they have generated, or the number of peer-reviewed research articles that they have published.

There might be evidence of close engagement with an international institution. An individual may represent the views of other academics as a member of an international panel of experts.

In short, there are numerous ways in which engagement with an activity can help realise the collective achievement of an institutional/departmental target.

What is particularly important with academic staff, is the need to identify activities that relate to their work, in the way that they perform their work. Academic staff, in general, tend to resist micro-management, and can often be reluctant to engage with institutional targets.

However, the translation of operational targets into relevant academic activities can be productive in terms of performance management.

Here are some more examples of potential academic activities that could support realisation of the vision statement:

- international reputation for the high-quality provision of teaching and research;

- to prepare graduates for professional careers – proportion of students employed within 12 months of graduation;

- attract highly qualified academic staff with international esteem;

    - Proportion of staff that hold research qualifications;

    - Proportion of staff that are active researchers;

    - Number of peer-reviewed articles published per head;

- recognised as a leading contributor to educational, research and industrial partnerships;

    - Proportion of total income from funding grants/commercial projects/consulting arrangements/intellectual property licensing;

- significant social and economic impact;

    - Number of projects with voluntary sector;

- cultivating industrial projects;
  - Number of projects solicited per annum;
  - Total income received per annum from industrial projects;
- sustain a diverse set of income streams;
  - Percentage mix of recurrent teaching and research income, commercial research income, industrial projects and other income.

> **Reflection:** *How many of these could your staff successfully engage with tomorrow?*

This stage can be both exciting and sobering. You will see the potential of some staff that is not being fully utilised, but you may also realise that your vision is potentially not achievable with the current resources.

However, after considering the operational activities that could feed into a vision, you might also discover that different activities help you achieve your vision anyway.

> **Reflection:** *With support and development, what could be realised over the next twelve months? The next five years?*

Thinking even further into the future can give an added check as to the realism of a vision. You don't need to forecast an entire set of staff development plans for the department, but you could identify whether your vision will be achieved solely through staff development, or whether new staff will need recruiting.

If you are creating a vision for a departmental transformation, then it is wise to look at the student enrolment projections which should come from the central planning unit at the same time, as significant growth may affect your plans.

Exercise

Using the data that you have collected so far, construct a vision statement and measures profile for your own situation. Remember that you now have:

- Data from the *Awareness* component; some description of the current state relating to the internal assessment of the organisational unit/individual staff member, etc. For a department you will know what proportion of staff hours are spent on teaching, research and administration for instance.

- Data from the *Definition* component; you will have gathered external data that enables the position of the object that will be the subject of the transformation. For example, you will have data from the relevant league tables, student survey data that is reported externally, research assessments, etc.

Usually, when then the data is brought together, a more holistic picture forms. You begin to understand the character of the department, but you also begin to have a more informed view of your competitors since you are looking at their data as well in the *Definition* component.

Additionally, you will no longer be constrained by the measures that your HEI currently uses to measure performance. In the example above, the *"proportion of staff hours ... spent on teaching, research and administration"* is described.

You might decide that this, in conjunction with a financial income profile, may be the most concise means of reporting progress towards your vision.

Once you have constructed a vision and measures profile from the data you have collected, you are in a much better position to argue for its inclusion in your reporting.

Don't worry if you find that you need some more data to proceed. If that is the case, at least you know what to ask for!

The mere observation that data is missing indicates that you have a need for it to satisfy and justify the vision that you are creating.

Remember that you will spend a lot of time talking about your vision, so it is important that it's based on a solid footing of data.

11 TACTICS - ANALYTICS

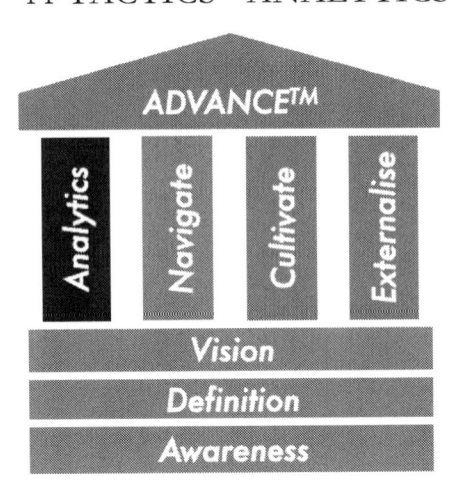

The *Analytics* component of ADVANCE helps us focus on understanding how to use measurements to their best effect. Lots of organisations produce data from their management information systems (MIS), and they spew out reports which are presented at meetings and other fora.

Organisations are complex entities and the breaking

down of the information that is produced helps us understand more detailed activities of the operations.

For example, a report that shows a trend of reducing student fee income does not explain the reasons for this trend occurring. It does provide the opportunity to pose the question:

"Why is this happening?"

Of course, a coaching manager might ask:

"What are the reasons for this trend?"

These questions will then initiate further scrutiny that may uncover a whole host of reasons such as (but not limited to):

- Reduction in enrolments;

- Increased number of student withdrawals;

- Different mix of fees for a given number of students, etc.

This process is what we generally understand as *analysis*, and is a daily occurrence as we unpick the broader measures to run the organisation.

So, how does *analytics* differ to analysis?

Analytics refers to the overall approach of discovering and interpreting insight from data, that is used to guide decision making. This guidance may include scenario modelling, that incorporates predictive modelling to aid understanding of the current and future situations.

A large part of analytics is the process of communicating the insight by incorporating visualisation techniques, but also it is the use of these techniques that help elicit meaningful patterns, leading to potentially new knowledge.

From a practical perspective, the current state of analytics is a marriage between statistics and computer science, which not only provides the necessary analysis and predictions, but also to automate the repetitive scenario modelling on generally large and distributed datasets. A lot of this activity originated under the banner of *Operations Research* (OR).

We are not going to dive into the technicalities here; there is a vast base of literature that deals with the mechanics of analytics.

We use the *Analytics* component to focus on the identification, maintenance and consumption of data to inform better decision-making, so that the outcomes can be realised. *How will the data help you?*

Here are a few scenarios that may resonate with you:

- There is insufficient data upon which to base a decision. *"We don't know how many unique visitors there are to our website because it's managed by a third party"*.

- The time taken to obtain the data is too long. *"We can't hang around to wait for reports, that then need to be analysed and cross-referenced."*

- The data is inaccessible. *"We must have the data, but it isn't available through the XYZ system."*

Having identified your vision, together with the key measures, you'll be in a much better position to know what data you will need.

Sometimes our enthusiasm for improvement clouds our thinking and we rush off and develop comprehensive reporting systems that collect and harvest both the data we want, as well as data that will not help us reach our objectives.

Analytics is about determining the actual data, analysis and forecasting that is required, and then ensuring that existing mechanisms are fully exploited.

Only when an existing system cannot deliver what is required do we consider changes; in most cases the existing systems can deliver sufficient data to support enough modelling to make significant improvements.

In the case of using ADVANCE for individuals, this phase is particularly useful. We can find it difficult to measure our own development and it is not always intuitive (or even attractive!) to seek data from others.

However, the realisation that external data sources are useful means that individuals start actively soliciting feedback on their performance as a result of ADVANCE, as they can see a faster way forward.

Value

Back in the Introduction, we posited that *"it's all about the people"*.

A lot of performance management systems concentrate upon *process*, which is understandable to some degree as processes are normally easy to quantify and monitor. If students receive feedback in two weeks rather than four, then a reduction in the lead-time can be reported.

Of course, it does not follow that a student will view this as an improvement. The feedback may be of lower quality and less detailed, or it may be judged to be too generic across the cohort.

So we have to be careful that not only do we collect the correct data, it has to be of sufficient quality, volume and breadth to permit further analysis.

Businesses commonly refer to *stakeholder value*. Does a student/employee/employer/society (stakeholder) receive a fair return (value) from a university?

If we focus intently on the value that students obtain from their experience of study, there would be a concerted effort to define measures that relate directly to specific operational activities; in other words to understand and monitor the organisational processes that students interact with (sometimes referred to as 'the student journey').

A focus upon the value of staff might concentrate upon finding ways of acquiring data about staff, so that management decisions can be made relatively quickly rather than relying upon an annual staff survey.

> **Reflection:** *From the data you gathered during the Awareness component, what measures does your organisation have in place to monitor the value obtained by your stakeholders?*

As-is, to-be

As leaders we are interested in the future ('to-be'), but we also recognise that we need to know how far aware the vision is from the current situation ('as-is'). Our key questions therefore are:

- *What is the current situation ('as-is')?* Having completed the strategy phase of ADVANCE you'll have a comprehensive set of data that includes not only quantitative measurements of performance, but also the location and detail of the various institutional repositories. During the process of discovering this data, you'll no doubt have made some new acquaintances that will help you in the future.

- *What challenges are on the horizon that could be avoided?* At this point you should have a combination of data sources. First, the external data that you gathered as part of the *Definition* phase will give you a perspective on the wider sector that your department/institution operates within. Second you will have already synthesised your own thoughts and experience together with the views of people you work with. Many coaches and attendees of my workshops have remarked that their daily conversations have now much more value, since they are using the insight that they gain from regular data-gathering to inform the questions they pose. 'Open questions' are a great assistance as well.

- *Are all the critical issues being monitored appropriately?* One of the dangers of investing effort into the future is that the essential operations are neglected in some way, resulting in a reduced quality of service. This can be one of the most challenging aspects of any transformation, as some mistakes can be catastrophic enough to question the need for a particular change initiative. When a culture needs to change, it is not always a good idea to partition some staff as caretakers while you lead all the exciting work. Everybody needs to be encouraged to participate, and therefore we have to be sure that the daily business will only be improved, not harmed. A clear focus on stakeholders is important; it reinforces who staff are serving and is a constant reminder of the essential activities for legal/regulatory compliance. Management systems that focus on stakeholders tend to be more successful in this regard, and we should endeavour to choose measures that help us drive improved behaviours. You'll find that the data gathered during the *Awareness* component is useful here.

- *What are the priority actions?* Priority actions fall into two categories. First, there are actions that are visible from basic report analysis; *what needs to happen with regard to a drop in student achievement?* Second, what actions are there that affect our ability to reach strategic objectives? For example: *What is the key factor affecting student recruitment in this subject discipline?*

- *Where is the detail for further analysis?* This question ensures that we collect all of the information that we need to be able to inform our decisions. It's of no use to collate aggregated data for reporting, if we cannot dis-aggregate to understand the underlying causes.

Use these questions as your own, regular 'sense-check'.

Their simplicity disguises incisiveness, particularly when posed by a coaching manager!

Reporting and visualisation

The prevalence of desktop PC business software such as spreadsheets, together with in-built tools to quickly assemble graphics has resulted in lots of creativity being applied to organisational reports. Please do resist the temptation to use every available graph in each report. If we assume that we are only going to present information of value, then there are two basic rules to abide by as follows:

- The measures should be accompanied by a graph that indicates the trend. Graphs referred to as 'Dot Plots' are the simplest and most desirable.

- A value to reflect the variance since the last report. This can either be a positive or negative number, or arrows can be used for a graphical visualisation.

Many reports have considerable variations in this theme, but in essence you should strive for simplicity. An added benefit is that their simplicity means that local statistics departments will be able to produce them quickly. Anything that communicates the data and insight faster is a good thing.

Frequency

As leaders we are of course interested in our staff. Our use of a coaching mindset means that we see the value of developing our staff, and in return our staff will perform at a higher level.

Since conversation is a fundamental part of coaching relationships, a scenario can develop whereby the person doing the coaching has the broadest view of the staff values and behaviour, but not everyone else has the privilege of sharing that view.

In time, as a culture develops, the values and behaviours of staff will develop and higher performance will become the norm. But what should we do in the meantime?

It might be that there are some issues that are not being surfaced by staff, even to a coaching manager, and then by implication those difficulties are not being attended to. This can lead to extra inertia for the change initiative to overcome.

> **Reflection:** *Compare the student feedback of teaching with your assessment of the module teaching team's satisfaction in their roles. What do you observe?*

Universities often survey their staff anonymously on an annual basis, and report back the cumulative results. In a similar vein, the UK HEIs conduct a National Student Survey (NSS) to understand the satisfaction of students in relation to a number of factors such as teaching quality, assessment and feedback, Student Union, etc.

The use of the NSS results (which are made public for all HEIs) to manage performance has resulted in institutions installing their own student feedback systems.

What are the reasons for this?

One reason is that it is difficult to monitor performance based upon an annual measure. How can those delivering the student experience understand what really improves the reported student satisfaction with such an infrequent measure?

As a result, some HEIs measure student satisfaction

more frequently at the end of each semester or term, so that dissatisfaction can be discovered earlier and corrective actions can be taken.

Another reason cited is that students can sometimes be reticent to commit their true feelings to a written survey, and that more practice in completing surveys, and more evidence that action will be taken as a result of completing the survey, will improve the quality of data collected.

Similarly, you wouldn't check application figures annually, as there are some marketing and outreach activities that could positively affect the recruitment cycle. So, if we are interested in our staff, we should place data gathering with respect to how valued they feel, as a priority activity.

Whether you do this more formally using an anonymous questionnaire or not is a matter for you, your culture and your bureaucracy. But as a coaching manager you understand the benefit of engaging directly with your staff to develop their capabilities and talents.

If you develop a reflection habit that is structured, it is wise to include data from conversations you have with staff.

This is best achieved by carrying a notebook with you at all times (many of you will already), so that you can jot down the essence of a conversation you have with each individual.

It isn't usually necessary to record exactly who it was, or where it happened, but a brief note can capture the current sentiment, that might otherwise be lost in the busy-ness of the day.

As is so often the case with reflection habits, it's the process of data capture that assists your memory. Your act of noting a thought down somehow reinforces it, and also permits you to reflect in the moment. You also have a record that can be entered into your structured reflection system.

Being critical

Part of the practice of a coaching manager is the ability to ask good questions. In fact, like good educators, coaching managers *"don't teach answers, they teach questions"*.

The same approach should be applied to the data we discover, and the data we receive. Data, and particularly reports, can mis-lead through error. Organisational politics can result in data being presented in specific ways to exaggerate or conceal poor performance. How do we deal with this?

The best antidote to errors (and there will always be errors) is to practice excellent data hygiene and process integrity yourself, and act upon the insight you discover.

For you to act with integrity, whilst using data produced by somebody else, means that you need to assure yourself that the data has been collected properly.

Tread carefully when questioning the origin of data or results of analysis; people can fell threatened and become defensive, particularly if the debate is public.

Questions about the data tend to relate to statistical concepts of reliability, sample size and bias. For instance:

- What is the standard deviation of this value?

- What is the significance of the variance?

- Is there a seasonal/cycle in the results or is it just noise?

- How representative was the training set of data for the model?

- What bias might exist in the sample?

- What was the sample size?

- What confidence do you have in the forecast?

Other questions around visualisation are important to query, particularly if the comprehension of reports is difficult. Visualisation standards can be challenging to adopt at the beginning, so the sooner you establish that trend plots are preferable to tabular data, and that pie charts don't really tell us much, the sooner you will all benefit from analytics reporting.

Such systems can bring new dimensions to meetings, where you spend some time looking at the outcome data (which reports what has already been actioned upon), and the majority of the time looking forward and discussing future scenarios that are based upon performance data.

Yet more opportunities to coach!

Exercise

If you are reading this book before you have started to implement ADVANCE, it is a useful exercise to answer the five questions in 'As-is, to-be' (p104). Keep your answers safe and then repeat the exercise when you have completed *Awareness, Definition* and *Vision*.

RICHARD HILL, PhD

One way to approach the *Analytics* component of ADVANCE is to select a particular area of concern for analysis, and through further questioning, analysis and dialogue with those around you, develop a focus that makes explicit use of the data to initiate small-scale improvements. For example, student retention is an important factor that affects the health of a programme, department or institution.

Traditional approaches would look at the withdrawal figures, interview a few students, and then spend a lot of time hypothesising about what we think are the reasons. A more analytics based approach might be to look at a broader set of student data and then produce some measures that your analysis indicates could be related to a student's choice to withdraw.

This might be their achievement or engagement with lectures, and you might also look at personal tutor meeting records. Further analysis might indicate that students of a particular demographic are more likely to withdraw, which would help identify where support efforts could be channelled.

Using the measures from your *Vision*, populate each metric with the data from your current situation. This is your baseline from which all subsequent activities will be measured.

Depending upon the effort that is required to obtain the data, you might need to create a protocol that simplifies this in the future, such as a request to the IT department to create a report of the data that you need for your purposes. These can sometimes take a little time to arrange, but once they are done they are embedded in the system.

12 TACTICS - NAVIGATE

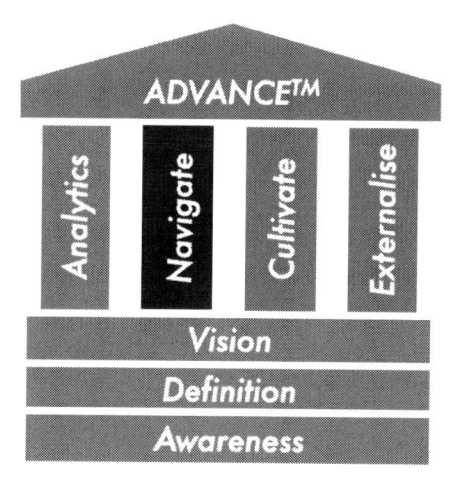

Navigate reflects the decisions that we take to utilise existing methods, systems or processes to bring our goals to fruition. For instance, you may have identified a number of potential of areas to develop in your organisation, each area being measured or influenced by a number of institutional processes or systems. Important questions at this juncture could be:

- When faced with a number of choices, which process or collection of processes will deliver what you require?

- Which system owns the data you need to move towards your vision?

- Who owns the data/system/process?

Even experienced managers are not familiar with a lot of the system complexities in HEIs. There are just too many disparate systems to look at and it is unlikely that you will come into direct contact with them all unless a concerted effort is made.

ADVANCE may have already prompted you to investigate a system that is new to you, but is actually an established part of your environment.

It might be the case that a system provides data to someone, who passes the result onto you. This 'insulation' means that you have never interacted directly with the underlying system, and therefore you are not fully aware of what its capabilities are. As a coaching manager, that will hopefully change.

Key concerns

Your ability to navigate the systems in your institution means that you need to have a holistic overview of what exist. Fundamentally, you need knowledge of:

- The data and planning cycles;

- The decision making structures - committees, working parties, etc.;

- What reports are produced, and what data they use (is it three months old for example, or do the numbers include Home/EU students only?);

- The culture and politics. Can you obtain the data from multiple sources/places? How consistent is the data from those sources?

Start from the top and work your way down, otherwise it will be a much bigger task than it need be.

Data and planning cycles

You will be probably find information on your organisation's data and planning cycles on your corporate intranet, or failing that by speaking to your central planning and quality assurance departments.

The data cycle is the superset of processes that gathers data about students and financial information. It includes data such as:

- Applications and enrolments;
- Withdrawals;
- Student demographics;
- Student surveys;
- Student results and achievement;
- Teaching quality;
- Complaints.

Of course this is not an exhaustive list, and the data

captured varies between institutions in terms of the actual sub-systems, but the overall result is eventually the same. The repositories that make up the data cycle each have calendars of capture and reporting frequency, that are locally used to define and report on performance indicators.

For instance the system will record the number of student withdrawals, but a localised report will show a retention figure that is calculated and used as a management measure.

Another example is that of 'health checks'; the data is collected and utilised for the purposes of assessing the performance of a course, subject or department in relation to internal targets such as financial viability.

Your central planning unit will have oversight of the planning cycle, in which the institution's performance against strategic objectives is measured, as well as the creation of planning targets for the future.

This cycle relies heavily on the data collected as part of the data cycle, which is sometimes a revelation for those managers who take the view that they are at the mercy of the planners.

The reality is that the planning unit acts upon the information that is generated by the operations, which in turn populates the repositories through the data cycle.

Planning functions can often be perceived as difficult, inflexible units to deal with, especially if you try to use argumentation to change their perspective.

One of the reasons that they appear this way is because of their reliance and absolute focus upon the data. If you want to change the institution, you need to identify the key datasets that will influence the decisions of the planning unit.

Localised processes

But what about more local processes? There are lots of opportunities to lead change by using existing mechanisms, and there are many opportunities to bring a change management initiative to a halt by ignoring them.

An academic department may be concerned with the general levels of student achievement. Perhaps an analysis of final year modules (prompted by the *Analytics* component) has identified that students are not performing as well as the sector at large.

Rather than just instigating a mechanism to report student achievement, the coaching manager looks for additional actions to take that will not only perform the diagnosis, but will also help improve the overall performance in the future.

> **Reflection:** *Which processes/systems/committees have the power to positively affect the student experience of a module?*

Since the academic coach has a raised awareness of their surroundings, they are better placed to see existing institutional processes in different, positive ways.

How many times have you chosen not to utilise the 'minor modification' process because of the paperwork?

When was the last time you saw the quality enhancement committee as an opportunity to proactively change a module to improve student attainment?

These questions help us re-frame what the purpose of committees are, and ultimately, what value they can provide us if we re-engage with a coaching mindset.

Remember also that effective leadership is about setting the example; when those around you observe your strategic use of localised processes to effect positive change, they'll start to adopt the practice as well, which is one step nearer to a culture that coaches high performance.

Exercise

Your data gathering so far will already have introduced you to systems that you previously were unaware of. You should now look more proactively for systems that will provide the services that you will require to increase your influence. There are two key activities to undertake now:

Activity One: Familiarise yourself with your organisaton's data and planning cycles.

For the data cycle, construct a calendar of key data gathering events. You may find that your institution already compiles this and publishes it. Typical data might include:

- Date of the event, e.g. November;

- Data collected, e.g. Survey of student leavers;

- Purpose of collection, e.g., to identify quantitative statistics for reporting of withdrawals, and qualitative reasons for students decisions around leaving their courses;

- Audience, e.g. Internal for performance

measurement and also for external agencies such as the Higher Education Statistics Agency (HESA).

For the planning cycle, this will mean gathering the following data:

- The planning document, e.g., Strategic plan;

- The range of the planning view, e.g., 5 years;

- The constitution of the plan, e.g., Colleges/Faculties/Departments/Schools and their strategic concerns;

- Who authors the planning document, e.g., Governing council, university executive, Deans, Heads of Department, etc.;

- Who monitors the plan, e.g., Planning unit, university executive;

- Who is the audience, e.g., internal or public.

Activity Two: Construct your own table of requirements for data that includes the systems and that provide the necessary data. For each system that provides data, identify the owner of that system, together with an associated committee that can effect change.

For example, you may receive reports that student performance is declining. The owner of the report is the statistics unit, which extracts data from the Assessments and Awards unit.

Assessments and Awards reports data as provided from the assessment methods as identified by the module descriptions approved by the Quality Assurance department.

The only opportunity to change assessment practices is therefore to use the minor modification process by engaging with the local Quality committee.

Knowing that this is the case, you can now identify the calendar for minor modification submission and then fix a point on your calendar that identifies a point in time by which module teaching reviews have to be completed by. If this date is missed, the opportunity is lost for one academic cycle.

You can use this as a prompt to initiate the appropriate discussions with staff around the performance of their students.

13 TACTICS - CULTIVATE

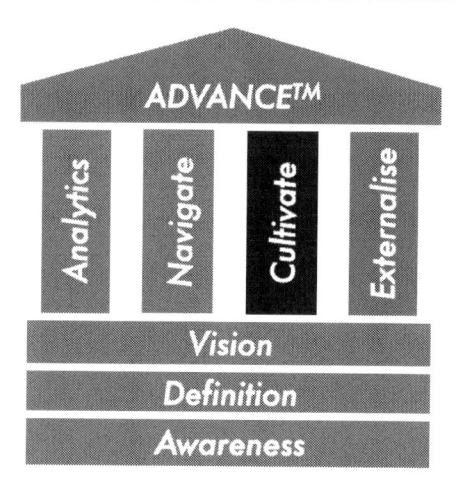

In agriculture, cultivate makes us think of preparing the soil for planting and tending to crops. When we cultivate we improve something; we foster growth, perhaps by focusing on a particular situation, person or characteristic.

To achieve change that lasts, we are going to have to cultivate those around us (and probably ourselves at the same time). ADVANCE requires us to use data to improve the quality of the decisions we make.

But we can't rely on the decision-making of one leader, as there is insufficient capacity and capability to undertake the busy operations of a department or institution.

We also know that the academic environment is full of people with a leadership mindset; they want to lead or be led; they don't warm to directive management.

We therefore need to build a culture that increases leadership capacity, so that more individuals are empowered to take the initiative, but also to ensure that they take initiatives that will move the department forward, not strangle it with uncoordinated conflict.

As you will have read in the previous chapter, we don't necessarily have to create new processes every time we want to initiate change. Some managers do this and create longer term problems for themselves.

Often it's best to make better use of the existing systems and processes; you might use them in different ways, or increase the value of them. But the key is to save any disruption for specific obstacles.

Culture change, and the processes of cultivating a different group mindset are complex topics. We are not going to address this complexity in its entirety in one chapter of a book.

However, we are going to explore a fundamental instrument of most organisations - the annual staff appraisal - and examine how a coaching mindset, combined with rational data from the environment, can significantly accelerate your ability to cultivate positive change.

Annual appraisals

The annual staff appraisal can strike dread/apathy/excitement/disappointment into all parties. In many cases, staff may feel that they will have to defend what they have done, or at least make an argument to counter what their manager expects from them.

As discussed earlier in Chapter 5 (p30), there is a tension between coaching as a developmental activity, and appraisal, which is something that a coaching manager must navigate carefully.

Managers might want to use appraisal processes and documentation for the purposes of 'transparency' – where everyone appears to be set common objectives that can be easily reported on. Inevitably, with such a situation it is difficult to get all staff to play to their strengths. We are all different, and have something unique to offer.

Managers are also being 'managed', and therefore they are likely to be required to report when all of their staff appraisals have been completed (are all the forms completed correctly and filed with HR?).

If you have a few appraisals left to do, and they should have been completed earlier, there may be an implicit pressure to 'get the paperwork done', rather than fully take advantage of a developmental conversation with a member of staff.

In a university setting there is the additional challenge of working with academic staff. As academics we like to argue and debate; we like to understand what something really means, and feel that we can relate to the context upon which a measure might be applied.

We don't have a problem with qualitative measures, but the fact that we are comfortable with the fact that we don't have an answer readily available, doesn't necessary help the organisation progress.

But academic life can be a relatively selfish pursuit, and if we are thinking, we are learning. As we have explored earlier in this book, academic staff in general respond less enthusiastically to directive management styles, hence our advocacy of the manager as a coach.

But as leaders we should attempt to focus upon activities that deliver value. What is the point of maintaining a dysfunctional approach to staff appraisals, if the mere thought of it saps the life out of us?

However, if you think that you can just dispense with appraisals, then good luck. It would be a bold move to counter the generally accepted wisdom of a large bureaucracy, that has policies for staff appraisals, even though most of the managers see it for what it is.

Of course as leaders we shall tap into our optimism and explore a more positive approach.

> **Reflection:** *Reflect upon the conversations that you have had with staff in relation to their performance at appraisal time. Now compare this with your daily conversations. What differences do you observe? How can you transform the annual appraisal conversation with a member of staff?*

Perhaps the first issue to tackle is that the appraisal might typically be an annual conversation, and therefore it is too detached from working life. So maybe the first thing to think about is how the annual appraisal can be coupled more directly into the daily conversations.

How can daily dialogue contribute towards the annual appraisal?

What departmental themes could link a staff member's contribution into the departmental/institutional vision?

If we are going to evaluate performance, what evidence would you expect a member of academic staff to provide?

These questions are much easier to answer if we have a clear vision of what the department/institution will look like, which you will have as a result of the foundation stones of ADVANCE.

You will have the confidence that not only is the vision based upon reason and fact, but you will also have involved the same staff who you are appraising during its construction.

If, after all this they don't know what the vision looks like, how can they translate your aspiration into their daily working lives?

This should give you a clear idea of who falls into the 'un-coach-able' club.

As I said earlier, don't waste energy coaching staff who aren't receptive to open, challenging, developmental language. Invest in those who have potential, and those who are already performing at a high level.

When you have developed your vision based upon facts that are relevant to your environment, the future is crystal clear. You will have identified the measures/metrics/characteristics that will indicate progress towards your vision. You can feel the future success!

If a staff member can't 'feel' the success, maybe they are a) in the wrong role, or b) in the wrong environment.

You need to exercise some sensitivity in both of these cases. I feel that directive performance management can often ignore these two scenarios (or at least dismiss them, assuming that if someone is truly unhappy they'll find another job), resulting in frustration for the manager and undue stress and anxiety for the staff (and their families, significant others, etc.).

If you remember from Chapter 5, a coaching manager has to have the mindset whereby they truly want to help people. That includes people who don't seem to be able to align themselves with the vision. Maybe they have been used to a way of being managed, and your approach is a surprise.

Or they are actually quite fearful of change. Coaching can be quite effective in these situations, particularly if you commit to developing relationships based on trust.

They need to trust that you are genuinely interested in their workplace well-being. You can only build this trust by being optimistic, honest and generous with them. So, perhaps they are not quite 'un-coach-able' yet.

Attendees at my workshops have echoed this sentiment many times; through a coaching oriented relationship they have helped a staff member either align themselves better with a department, or they have worked together to discover what the individual would prefer to do.

When a staff member has a clear vision of what they want, a lot of the barriers disappear. Whilst this may result in the member staff leaving, their departure is because they have found something better *for them*.

Don't underestimate the strength of the message that this projects to the immediate environment. When staff leave of their own accord 'for something better', they leave on positive terms.

The rest of the department will see this; they will already know that a particular individual would not align with the change initiative.

But they also observe an academic manager who reinforced the belief that the staff should be valued, and that means helping them discover their own potential, through a role they are suited to.

The coaching manager does not persecute staff and make them perform against their will.

So, with your measures and vision to hand (which you repeat and make reference to at every opportunity), the daily conversations become easier.

It's then a process of aligning individual staff capabilities with the departmental themes. It's about identifying where staff development has to take place – and after a short while, your staff will start telling you what development they need to align with your vision.

As a departmental culture develops, mindful of a clearly articulated vision, the annual appraisal becomes more straightforward.

Staff will identify the evidence that is already in place as a result of them aligning themselves to the vision. The developmental conversations will already have started during the year, and will be regarded as continual.

The appraisal will suddenly have found its place – a

chance to review progress over an extended period, and an opportunity to think a year or two ahead, as well as to discuss individual staff aspirations. Therefore, the appraisal will have morphed into something that is more *developmental*.

And this is at the heart of being able to *cultivate* a culture that wants to continually perform at a higher level.

OK you say, this is all well and good. But at the outset there are staff who will find this approach challenging, and they will make the process arduous. Surely this will bring the whole culture change to a halt?

It is common for the first round of appraisals to be difficult. There will be a minority that welcome the change in approach, fully subscribing to the notion that they can take charge of their own development in the context of improving the department.

There will be a significant portion that are wary, suspicious, and genuinely frightened that they can't measure up to the vision. Some of them will display apathy (*"I've seen this before; just sit tight until the next initiative"*), some will retreat and become reclusive, and some will generate a veil of enthusiasm, and produce a shopping list of expensive, time-consuming staff development activities.

Beware, because the first request that you turn down could be used as an excuse to suggest that you never really meant what you said in the first place!

And finally there is likely to be a hardcore minority who have every intention of not engaging. They may be frightened, confused, delusional, incompetent or just insecure. Every trick in the book will be used to dodge the process.

Some managers see this as a game, with the objective of trying to 'outwit' their 'opponents'. Unfortunately there are many examples of this approach being legitimised, in that the measured performance improves.

Of course in such situations it is unlikely that a longer term vision has been created and it is the short-term transformation of numbers that is reported as a success. Nonetheless, the cost to the environmental culture can be quite damaging.

As an academic coach you'll persevere beyond the initial challenge as you'll have confidence in the long term view. The measures you will have chosen will be based on the data that you have reasoned is important.

In time, some of the hardcore will come around and realise that it might be interesting to engage after all, especially since the manager seems to want to help staff.

The second round of appraisals is where managers see the greatest transformation. The keen early adopters are already bearing fruits of their focused engagement, and doing things that are visible to the rest of the department.

They'll already be in a position to *Externalise* (Chapter 12). Success in acquiring one or two small funded projects can do wonders for the self-confidence, motivation and external visibility of an academic, which of course you will be supportive of.

While hard-liners will still be resisting, the rest of the department will have started shifting. They'll have witnessed the successes of the early adopters, and some will have got themselves involved already.

Others will test the water by suggesting some new

activities that they would like some development for. Some will be bold enough to set themselves a target to achieve for the coming year.

By the third appraisal the bulk of the changes will have been made. Staff will have discovered what they like doing, to what extent it can be accommodated (usually the department is more flexible than people think), and have witnessed the benefits to them personally, all wrapped up in a department that is performing better.

If during this period your department has recruited new staff, then the transformation is accelerated significantly. The new starters come in fresh and adopt the developmental approach without being held back by any prior cultural baggage.

What is important to remember is that if you actively monitor and measure performance in a directive way, the annual appraisal will remain the key event on the calendar to report achievement.

In contrast to this, a coaching-oriented style positively supports development on a continual basis, meaning that the annual 'check-in' can be more focused upon the strengthening of core values and the development of longer term career goals for an individual.

So, you have it within your power to re-purpose the staff appraisal process and it's an excellent instrument to cultivate higher performance.

> **Reflection:** *What are the potential benefits of planning to develop role models in your environment? What can staff learn from a role model?*

Exercise

A key tool of culture change is how you approach the appraisal and development of others. To do this you must familiarise yourself with the current staff appraisal process.

Sometimes this is referred to as a 'cycle', or a 'developmental review' and there may be key points in the annual calendar at which point certain activities are undertaken.

Once you have oversight of the process, look for ways in which your *Vision* and measures can be incorporated into the cycle. For instance, do you have an event whereby a line manager discusses the objectives of the department for the coming academic year?

As a coaching manager you are more likely to use these departmental objectives as prompts for developmental requirements for the individual concerned.

If all staff need to produce two published outputs this year, what support will each of them need? Some will need more support than others.

Depending upon your procedures for appraisal, you need to either rework the forms/processes etc., for your own purposes, or you should provide an addendum that enables explicit links to be drawn between the departmental/institutional objectives, and the individual's developmental requirements.

The purpose of the addendum is to explicitly highlight the linkage between an individual's contribution to the larger environment. This helps everybody by making clear what needs to happen, and prompts them to think about the support they need to help the department achieve its target.

Developmental conversations that start with this tend to productive. Sometimes an individual will not feel able to respond; this is OK as well, as the process of helping them complete it is another fantastic coaching opportunity.

If we look at some extracts from a developmental objective setting form (Tables 2 and 3), we can observe the link between departmental target, an indicator of what successful achievement looks like, a space for he individual's contribution as to how they shall engage, and a date by when it needs to be concluded.

This both prepares the groundwork and frames a coaching conversation in terms of the individual's development. The key question for the individual is:

"What development support do I need to achieve my objectives?"

You might choose to add this to your form, to be completed as an outcome from your meeting.

THE ACADEMIC COACH

Dept. target	How will we know when this has been achieved?	How will you provide evidence of your engagement?	By when?
Improve student satisfaction score across modules taught	85% of the students will report 'satisfied' or 'very satisfied'		End of Semester
Improve first-time pass rate	80% of the students will pass first time and progress		End of Semester
Improve student attainment	60% of students achieve at least 2:1 or First		End of Semester
Provide timely, constructive written feedback to students	100% of summative assessment feedback received within 4 weeks of submission deadline		End of Semester

Table 2. Extract from the teaching quality section of a development review form.

Dept. target	How will we know when this has been achieved?	How will you provide evidence of your engagement?	By when?
Improve quality and volume of research output for the department	**Principal researcher:** 2 peer-reviewed articles, >3* **Researchers:** 3 peer-reviewed articles, >2* **Other staff:** 1 peer-reviewed article, >2*		End of year
Improve the external esteem of the department	**Principal Researchers:** 2 research events organised/ed. books/edited journal special issues **Researchers:** 1 research event organised/ed. books/edited journal special issues		End of year
Improve the research environment	**Principal Researchers:** attract and supervise 1 new PhD student **Researchers:** attract and supervise 1 new PhD student		End of year

Increase research funding into the department	**Principal Researchers:** achieve at least one successful bid >£50k as Principal Investigator **Researchers:** submit at least 2 applications for funding >£10k **Other staff:** engage with at least 1 funding bid submission		End of year

Table 3. Extract from the research section of a development review form.

Using the above as a guide, take the measures you identified in *Definition* and *Vision,* and create a document that can be used to augment your existing developmental review/appraisal documentation.

14 TACTICS - EXTERNALISE

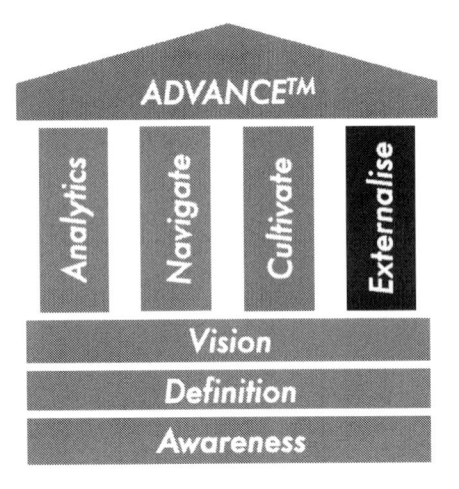

Success is rarely a solitary achievement. At all stages of a transformation there is a need to solicit support from colleagues, managers, and relevant communities of interest, either within an organisation or externally.

Once we recognise that external support can enable rather than hinder, we need to understand how that power can be harnessed to our advantage.

The approach used to advertise both our intentions and progress can be a great influence upon the eventual results of an initiative. How can messages be crafted to maximise impact with the intended audience?

In an academic setting, branding is related to the reputation that is recognised outside of the institution. What methods can you use to develop a brand/reputation?

> **Reflection:** List some activities that you could use to promote a brand. How many of these activities relate to your typical workday?

Build a brand

The question of branding is an interesting topic for higher education. What actually does it mean to 'brand' an academic or a department?

In the commercial sector, we would expect a branding exercise to enable a product, product line or service to be distinguishable from a competitor's offering. As such, an effective brand is a key asset, though its lack of tangibility means that you won't find it in the company accounts.

What then for universities? Unlike most commercial organisations, universities have a vast breadth to their offering. They're all in the same business – teaching and research – and even though the income proportions differ between research-intensive and teaching-intensive institutions, there are significant similarities.

Undoubtedly, there is evidence of strong branding, which tends to be a combination of excellent reputation for knowledge generation and dissemination, together with a lengthy heritage. In the higher education world, longevity cannot be bought.

But then we do have the more enterprising universities, that until recently were classified as the '94 Group'. Their heritage is embryonic next to Cambridge and Oxford, but they have established, strong brands that are clearly marketable.

What is apparent is that in the higher education sector, branding could appear synonymous with reputation. At this point, if you are working in an institution that has more recent history than the 16th century, then you might feel a little despondent.

This needn't be the case. If we see 'reputation' when we read 'brand', then why not think about how the external reputation of your department (your own profile or that of your staff) can be enhanced?

If we feel that a brand can be created, this can be an attractive proposition as departments that successfully recruit students onto highly regarded programmes demonstrate. In isolation, reputation-building efforts will not transform the reputation of an entire institution, but success is infectious, and it can be an effective way of re-branding.

One way to think about this is to let an institution's brand (reputation) emerge from the excellence that its departments can evidence, rather than relying on the imposition of a top-down brand.

Or, put another way, don't expect the marketing messages to constitute a brand in themselves. They are merely a vehicle to communicate a story of substance; the substance comes from your reputation.

So, let's assume that a) brand means (external) reputation, b) departments can change their reputation, and finally c) reputations are best built upon excellence.

How can we use the prospect of an excellent external reputation to drive improvement?

It comes back to *Vision*. The vision that we hold about what the department will look like in a future state.

The fact that more students will select our department as their first choice for a higher education experience.

The increase in privately funded projects that are attracted as a result of the department's presence in the market.

The way in which other institutions will talk about our department.

This vision requires an understanding of what the specific attributes will be, that characterise that new branding, as well as an understanding of the existing character of the institution in terms of what it feels capable of supporting.

For instance, if your institution is focused upon teaching, you're going to have a hard time becoming a research-intensive department overnight.

Similarly if your academic staff pull in 30% of the department's income thorough funding councils, and the teaching is delivered by PhD students, a focus on widening participation and reduction in entry tariffs is equally likely to be an uphill battle to start with.

However, the polarisation of a department's character does have one significant advantage; a relatively constrained effort can make your function distinct without appearing too contrarian. So, how might this look?

The key question to pose is how will external agents construct their views of the department. What are they likely to expect, and what can we give them?

The corporate answer to establishing or changing a brand is to use the marketing department. Many leaders report variable results with this approach and there are frequent complaints of marketing functions being too slow to react, or taking too much ownership of the messages to be propagated, to the extent that the intention of the original message is lost.

Fortunately the academic community has its own channels for the selling of a reputation. Academics traditionally publish their research, and travel beyond their home institution to deliver talks. This dissemination circuit has its own hierarchies, that vary between the subject disciplines.

Generally though, a peer-reviewed journal article and an invited keynote talk at a conference are regarded as 'good' reputation enhancers.

But aside from quality of output, there is also an element of quantity as well. The more external events that link back to academics from your department, the more 'buzz' will be generated.

Now be honest. Is your department really on the map when it comes to externality? Is this something you can get behind, using staff development processes to facilitate?

Here are some activities that help build departmental brands:

THE ACADEMIC COACH

- Academics professionally accredited by industrial bodies;

- Academics with research qualifications;

- Academics who blog and tweet about their projects;

- Academics who are members of advisory/standards boards;

- Course materials offered for free on the internet;

- Industrial associations/sponsorships for courses/students/prizes at graduation;

- Participation in regional regeneration projects;

- Creating spin-off companies;

- Hosting events for professional bodies;

- Open talks for the public;

- Greater quantities of small funding bids – spreading the name of the department further rather than concentrating on larger bids that are more competitive;

- Students given opportunities to attend academic conferences;

- Students publishing their work;

- Students excelling on industrial placements;

- Students blogging/tweeting favourably while

they're engaging in the above.

> **Reflection:** *How many of these activities do you/your staff engage in regularly?*

A lot of these become rather obvious when we make the conscious decision to establish a brand. The inevitable issue is finding the staff time to do it. As leaders we need to find mechanisms that can realise the latent value, and commonly the key instrument relates to your institution's academic workload planning system.

Your coaching conversations with staff will be reinforcing your story of the future state. Use your developmental mentality to ring-fence academic hours for development purposes, where they will have the greatest impact.

Another channel to influence is that relating to policy. What policies can you introduce, that will directly support an enhanced reputation?

> **Reflection:** *Consider the culture of your environment right now. What difference would it make if you only appointed academic staff with PhDs for instance? What possible impacts would this have? What opportunities would it create? What challenges would present themselves?*

Reputation requires us to think big, and implement now. Don't underestimate the effect of a multitude of small actions. Just make sure that they relate to your vision, and after a while your staff will do the rest for the department!

Exercise

Using your work from the *Definition* and *Vision*

components, think of all the activities that will support your strategic objectives.

From the example in Chapter 10 (p93):

"... The vision will be achieved by:

- *Delivering a high-quality portfolio that is relevant to the needs of industry;*

- *Creating a student experience that beats the sector median;*

- *Developing peer credibility amongst academic staff by increasing external activities;*

- *Creating and disseminating knowledge for social and economic benefit, both regionally and nationally."*

If we assume that a 'portfolio' is the collection of courses/programmes that a department offers, what evidence would you seek if you were to assess the quality? Perhaps you might look for:

- External accreditation from professional bodies;

- Favourable comments from external examiners/QAA;

- Stories of alumni who are working with recognisable employers;

- Employer endorsements;

- Student scholarships sponsored by employers;

- Excellent student achievement;

- Excellent student satisfaction.

Your data gathering will help identify the specific measures that characterise the sector you are operating in, and highlight what you and your competitors will be measured on.

From this you can quickly arrive at a set of activities that will help build a brand (reputation). For instance, the marketing department will have stories of selected student alumni that they use for promotional activities, but it is unlikely that they will renew the stories as frequently as you might be able to do.

How could you or your staff use stories that were more current and in greater volume?

More photos and quotes of ex-students can be powerful marketing collateral on both open days and on the web. Why not create a departmental alumni group on LinkedIn (or whichever social media service you prefer) and harvest more examples?

Prospective applicants (or their parents/guardians) are usually more interested in authentic stories rather than glossy leaflets, so showing them 30-odd examples of recent graduates pursuing exciting careers is a compelling tale to tell.

PART THREE

Part Three provides some additional resources to help you get started with the **ADVANCE** model, and also reviews what has been learned.

15 ADDITIONAL RESOURCES

The ADVANCE model will prompt you to look for tools and approaches to help you achieve your objectives.

Such is the flexibility of ADVANCE that you can incorporate tools that you are already familiar with, or introduce new techniques that are of particular interest. It is the process of collection, integration and review that is important.

Collect the data from various approaches in accordance with the requirements of each stage of ADVANCE, respect the overall ethos of establishing facts by undertaking systematic enquiry, and finally by adopting a coaching mindset you shouldn't go far wrong.

This chapter provides a brief list of resources that are useful for the HE sector, and it is likely that you will use them during the initial stages of data capture.

However, in addition, there is some further information with respect to the most frequent queries I receive either with coaches or training programme/

workshop attendees. These are:

- *Deeper reflection.* Having established a reflection habit: *"How do I extract even more value from the process?"*

- *Coaching through barriers.* As you adopt more coaching behaviours, you will start to come up against deeper seated resistance with some staff. *"How do I coach people through self-limiting beliefs?"*

ADVANCE welcomes experimentation and tailoring for your own environment. Just remember to record your experiments and reflect on the outcomes!

Resources

Finance and statistics

The Complete University Guide
http://www.thecompleteuniversityguide.co.uk/

The Guardian University Guide
http://www.theguardian.com/education/universityguide

Higher Education Information Database for Institutions (HEIDI)
http://www.heidi.ac.uk/

Higher Education Statistics Agency (HESA)
https://www.hesa.ac.uk/

An Insider's Guide to Finance and Accounting in Higher Education
Universities and Colleges Employers Association
http://www.ucea.ac.uk/en/publications/index.cfm/gtofinance

RICHARD HILL, PhD

Patterns and Trends in UK Higher Education 2015
Universities UK
http://www.universitiesuk.ac.uk/facts-and-stats/data-and-analysis/Pages/patterns-and-trends-uk-higher-education-2015.aspx

Research Excellence Framework 2014
http://www.ref.ac.uk/

UNISTATS
https://unistats.direct.gov.uk/

Reflection

Donald Schon, (1983) *The Reflective Practitioner: how professionals think in action.* London: Temple Smith
https://www.andrew.cmu.edu/user/skey/research_prev/reading/reflection_educational_role/et-schon.htm

Jenny Moon
http://www.cemp.ac.uk/people/jennymoon.php
http://www.cetl.org.uk/UserFiles/File/reflective-writing-project/ThePark.pdf

Deeper reflection

Those that practice regular reflection, and have an operational system in place, witness some significant benefits in their development.

At the very least, you will be more aware of how you behave – and while you might not always be pleased with the news – the increased accuracy of your insight will provide a more rigorous foundation on which to base your future decisions.

Many of those that have attended my leadership

development workshops have reported significantly larger successes as a direct result of adopting the reflection habit.

When I've coached clients, they also realise the potential of regular, structured reflection, and in the main this is sufficient to successfully achieve significantly higher than average performance.

However, there are two specific scenarios where the reflection habit needs to be extended. The first is when someone has been practicing reflection for some time.

They have got into the habit of setting developmental goals and using their deep reflection data to plan for new experiences.

The second scenario is when an individual presents a demanding goal that will have considerable impact; this may require 3-5 years to achieve, and substantial, sustained effort to successfully attain.

In such cases I tend to recommend adopting the reflection habit exclusively to begin with, but sometimes the time frame is so compressed that we need to add something else on top as well.

One of the important skills of reflection is the ability to separate the recording of facts from any interpretation that you might have 'learned' to use, to process the new experience.

This presents two key advantages for your leadership development:

- The 'significant' event is recorded accurately, with an emphasis upon fact. Which would you rather have to base your future decisions on – an account of a significant event seen through your normal 'prejudiced lens', or an accurate record of what actually happened?

- Since the recording of the event is separated from any reflection post-processing, the reflection itself is more significant. You consciously reflect upon the data that you have collected, safe in the knowledge that you have worked hard to ensure that the facts of the experience have been collected.

Furthermore, when you have completed the reflection, you have two records; the original event, and your subsequent, considered thoughts. This is invaluable when you start to look for patterns in your own behaviour.

I'm of the opinion that leadership is a continual learning process. We may coach others, but when we actively engage in reflection we are actually coaching *ourselves*.

But to qualify that specifically, it's a continual active *learning* process.

The reason I say this is that many people appear to be satisfied with passive learning through experience, measuring their progress in terms of years of service or the rung of the career ladder achieved.

I'm motivated to take charge of my learning, as I'm sure readers of this book are also.

You will already have started looking for new opportunities to engage in, either to practice your newly found skills, or to experiment with new experiences. This often occurs at a subconscious level, as I witness with clients in coaching sessions.

As they grow more aware of their progress, they start to actively plan for development experiences, further building their experiential evidence. As I mentioned earlier, this is enough of a development-boost for a lot of leaders, but if you really want to master your own development, we'll need to do a bit more.

Action planning

Action planning is useful when it is focused upon one, two, or at most three aspects of your development. It should be measurable (of course), used for a specific purpose, and discarded when the outcome has been achieved.

More importantly, it must be relevant to your current and future states, and is therefore shaped by the other development tools that you might employ.

Plenty of my workshop attendees complain about how difficult action planning can be, and that it seems to not be worth the effort as achieving a successful outcome can be sporadic.

It is likely that those who have not yet developed an accurate model of their self-awareness will find action planning problematic.

Sort out a reflection habit, and you'll have plenty of pertinent data to draw upon.

Finally, action planning needs to be considered part of a more holistic approach, but I'll come back to that in a short while.

A strong theme of my approach to behavioural changes for leadership development, is that any new habits should be simple to adopt. So my action plans tend to be lists of objectives.

Each objective is SMART (Simple, Measurable, Achievable, Result-oriented and Timebound). For more on SMART objectives please consult Professor Google.

But to be honest, the only aspect of SMART that my clients struggle with is *Achievable*.

It takes a fair bit of self-awareness to repeatedly assign yourself achievable goals (that mean something). Goals are either stratospheric, or just too safe.

Safe goals are achieved easily, but the lack of stretch does not promote effective personal development. If you're still unsure as to how to progress, establish the reflection habit right now.

So far, we have a process in place to capture experiential data and reflect upon it in a structured fashion.

We also have a simple means of expressing specific developmental objectives, with a focus upon delivery of outcomes. In the same way that structured reflection can be sufficient for many developing leaders, the addition of action planning, driven by themes that have emerged from the reflections, can provide added effectiveness.

But those who truly aspire to excel, can utilise their existing developmental habits to build a much more comprehensive, holistic system.

One of the potential limitations of capturing reflections and formulating action plans is that there could be a mismatch between what the individual pursues, as opposed to what is required for a given situation.

I feel that the risk of objective mismatch diminishes over time, as individuals become more self-aware. But therein lies the problem. If the risk diminishes the more you do it, then you are most at risk when you start the process.

As a result, I tend to coach clients to adopt the reflection habit as a primary, discrete activity, without being overly goal driven at the outset. Early on, it's more about self-discovery.

I've found that some people like a bit more structure to their learning when they start reflecting, and if they are used to a culture of action planning, then it's important to insure against any over-enthusiastic development plans being created.

In my experience, an effective approach is to tackle the issue of critical self awareness head-on, by asking the individual to conduct a self appraisal.

This needs to be quick and simple, to get the maximum benefit, and a SWOT (Strengths, Weaknesses, Opportunities and Threats) analysis can be a good starting point.

A better start, in my view, is a SWAIN (Strengths, Weaknesses, Aspirations, Inhibitors and Needs) analysis.

This approach contextualises current strengths and weaknesses in terms of the future desires of the individual, and implicitly fires up the relevant planning neurons.

Used at the outset, structured reflection can be suitably

constrained so as not to go too far off course, and the first set of developmental objectives are likely to be relevant to the initial self-assessment.

So what's the problem with adopting this whole system from day one?

Well, it can be done, but the danger is that it becomes too much of a system, that needs to be applied in a prescribed way. When faced with such a fundamental change in personal development, a lot of people cry out for forms and flowcharts, in order to cope with the amount of change.

This more or less guarantees its failure. Whilst we need to use paper (physical or virtual) to make records, we should not fall victim to excessive administration.

A developmental leader embraces the holistic view. If any gaps exist, they are plugged with efficient processes that enrich the overall development process. But the same individual is also acutely self-aware, and adopts an incremental approach to enhancing learning.

I favour such an approach when it comes to building a personal learning system.

First, build your self-awareness through regular, structured reflection. From the themes that emerge, use action planning to focus your attention on a constrained number of developmental issues.

Then, add the SWAIN self-appraisal checks to the mix.

Use each SWAIN to check your overall progress, and to diagnose any specific needs for your holistic development. In terms of frequency, you'll establish your own schedule. But here is a suggestion:

- Structured reflection – daily;
- Action planning – as and when development issues arise;
- SWAIN analysis – every quarter (3 monthly).

To obtain an overall view of your learning requires a suitable container, in which all of your learning evidence is 'kept'. Traditionally, artists keep evidence of their work in a portfolio, to illustrate how they have developed and to show what their capabilities are.

This is similar to what we might want, except that it would be useful if the path of learning development could be observed.

Journalling

The practice of journalling has been around for as long a people could write. If you develop a reflection habit, then you will need somewhere to record your experiences, draw conclusions and then plan your new experiments.

The experience of writing longhand can be cathartic. However, once the volume of entries starts to accumulate, it can become increasingly difficult to 'mine' your records to identify patterns.

Coupled with the fact that some people are worried that either a journal is lost, or that someone else might read it, there is often some resistance to writing things down.

A common reaction to the prospect of regular

reflection is: *"I couldn't possibly write down everything I feel, just in case it gets out"*. It's a shame that people feel this way, but I have two comments to make.

First, I am advocating reflection about how we develop as leaders, probably in the workplace. We are not talking about self-disclosure and deep therapy.

Second, if you don't want anyone else to read it, then there are methods that don't require you to keep your journals locked away in a safe.

Using technology

More people have access to technology these days, and for most university employees a computer is at the centre of their work. Computers can help with the reflection habit, since we have lots of opportunities to use them, particularly if you own a smartphone.

In Chapter 8 (p60) I shared my 'secret' to regular reflection:

Every workday I will write for a minimum of 10 minutes before I read my email.

I could, of course, be actually sending an email to myself, that contains my reflection. No financial outlay, the records are kept electronically so they can be searched, the organisation ensures that they are backed-up, and I can access them wherever I have access to a network connection.

This is the simplest and cheapest approach which is relatively secure. If you send the emails to another email address then you would have to ensure that they were encrypted before you sent them - emails are the equivalent of postcards on the Internet as everyone can read them - but if you send them to yourself, only the IT system administrator could read them.

Another alternative (which I do), is to use a free blogging service (such as Google Blogger, http://www.blogger.com, or Wordpress, http://www.wordpress.com) with the privacy controls set so that only the author (me) can see it.

The use of a blogging tool has significant advantages for your organisation. Table 4 below describes a workflow that will simplify your regular reviews. The simpler a tool is, the more you are likely to use it regularly.

Activity	Using a tool like Google Blogger (or Wordpress, etc.)
1. Collect - write notes at every opportunity, record fragments of conversations for later review.	Post frequently directly via the web, or through emails from your iPhone, internet cafe, PDA, etc. **At least 10 minutes per day before opening your email!**
2. Review and reject - go back and look at what you have written. Sort the wheat from the chaff. If you write one summary review every week, then that is at least 4 structured reflections per month. To review quarterly, you	Review your postings for the week. Write a summary post and *Label* it (different blogging platforms have different vocabularies - it might be *'tag'* or *'category'*). You might choose *weeklySummary* as your Label for instance. If you are reviewing the month

need only look at 3 of the latest monthly review postings.	then the label might be *monthlySummary*. And for quarterly reviews ... Why do I need to add a label? Labels allow you to quickly sort your postings. When you come to do your first monthly review you just click on the *weeklySummary* Label. Then just read the 4 latest postings and conduct your review.
3. Refine and plan - use the reviews to create stand-alone pieces of writing. For example, after writing for a few months you might want to write a summary piece of how a new approach you have adopted has developed over a semester. Now you can start to project forward and think about what you want to achieve with your writing.	Create a stand-alone post and label it 'article' or 'potential' or anything else that you can identify at a later date. Think of these posts as more developmental; if you have an idea that is related to this post, then use the Comments link at the bottom of the post to record your thinking. This is especially useful when developing a theme for your development.

Table 4. Workflow for reflecting with a web-based blogging tool.

At any point in time this tool serves as a snapshot of your current developmental needs, together with an explicit, reasoned narrative of your learning journey. It's also evidence of the importance that you place upon continued development. Coaching managers understand this and use reflective practice to develop themselves beyond all expectations.

Coaching through barriers

"If you knew you couldn't possibly fail, what would you try?"

This is a favourite staple of executive coaches, and for good reason. It strips away everything that inhibits your achievement, and gets you to focus on the outcome, exclusively.

An alternative could be:

"Let's say you do have enough time/money. Then what?"

Sometimes, when coachees are challenged they come too preoccupied with the question. What they need is a creative prompt to get them thinking a bit broader:

"Give me three options that would help move you forward."

When a coaching conversation appears to stall, you might actually be on the cusp of discovering the underlying reason for a barrier. It may be that the coachee is subconsciously waiting for you to bring the reason out into the open.

"What made you decide not to discuss this at the programme committee meeting? Talk me through your reasoning."

As a reflective practitioner yourself, you'll realise the

benefits of regular reflection. So why not use it to help remove an individual's self-limiting belief?

"I realise that you are finding working with Louise in Finance very difficult. But I'd like you to arrange to meet with her at some point over the next few weeks, and commit to writing down how you felt straight afterwards. Try and describe how you approached the situation, what you said, what the response was, and how it made you feel. What you write may help uncover the barrier."

This approach usually brings something to the surface, with the added benefit that the coachee will be doing this themselves and therefore there is further time for them to reflect before your next meeting. If they are still struggling, you can help with a more direct line of questioning as follows:

"How do you feel when you think about meeting with Louise? Which part of the conversation do you fear the most?"

Here are some indicators that a coachee has beliefs that are limiting them:

- *"This is going to very difficult."*

- *"**I don't** have sufficient experience to do this."*

- *"**I don't** have as much experience as John and he has much more esteem."*

- *"**I'll never** be able to work at that level."*

- *"It's always the same. **I can't** get funding."*

- *"No, there are much more qualified staff than me for that job."*

- *"**I have to** do this, otherwise what will the Dean think?"*

- *"**I need to** do better, but I'm not as confident as I used to be".*

Some key phrases are highlighted above **in bold**. People often say what they are thinking. If they can say *"I will"* instead of *"I have to"* or *"I want to"* instead of *"I have to"*, a lot of barriers to progress can be eliminated.

One of the benefits of adopting a coaching approach is that you help people to move on with their thinking, so that they can achieve more. You get to practice simple techniques and observe the results.

> **Reflection:** *When was the last time you said "I can't" or "I have to"? How might the situation have changed with alternative language?*

16 WRAP-UP

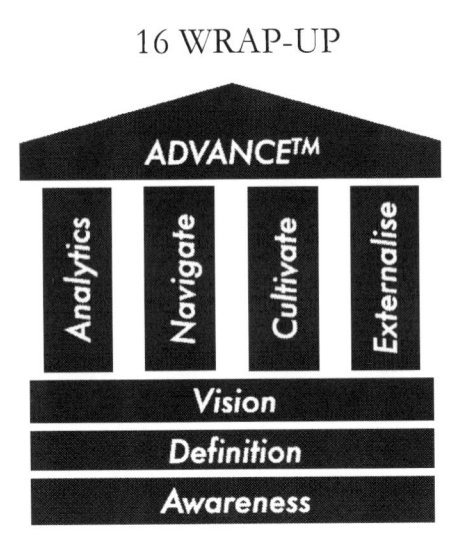

ADVANCE™

- Analytics
- Navigate
- Cultivate
- Externalise

Vision
Definition
Awareness

Let's review what we have covered.

In Part 1 of the book, we explored the changing HE environment in the UK as it moves into a competitive free-market. We looked at the concept of performance management and considered the challenges we face when talking about performance in academic environments.

Most HEIs have cultures whereby conversations about performance are more readily accepted in the administrative functions, as a consequence of more directive management styles. Academic functions, on the other hand are typically managed in a less directive way.

Coaching was introduced, as well as the specific concept of the 'coaching manager', which can be a way to lead the improvement of staff performance without resorting to directive management styles.

Finally, we looked at the collection and use of data to establish facts about the local and external environment, in order to provide the rigour for great decision-making.

In Part 2, the ADVANCE model was introduced, to guide the activities required to transform an individual, group or organisation. This commences with strategic phase, starting with a requirement to increase *Awareness*, through individual, group or organisational reflection. This involves the collection of local data that will help build a picture of the current stat from an internal perspective.

Data is then gathered from outside of the object to be transformed; this enables the individual/group to be positioned in relation to external bodies or competitors.

Once this has been completed, a *Vision* can be created that contains a narrative of the future, aspirational state, along with some relevant measures of success. This vision is a constant reminder of what success will look like, setting the scene for coordinated change and improvement.

Once the strategic phase has been completed, a series of tactical components are available to assist the realisation of the planned change. These components can be used in any combination, in any order, as and when the change initiative requires.

Measures of performance are identified at operational level, that directly support the overall measures in the *Vision* narrative. These measures concentrate on behavioural performance drivers, rather than numbers that confirm the action that has already taken place. Analysis of these measures, combined with subsequent modelling, enables future performance to be predicted and worked towards.

Existing processes are explored to ensure that they support the transformation, or to understand what modifications need to happen in order for them to provide the necessary support. Leaders will navigate the plethora of mechanisms, systems and committees to select the most effective processes for change.

Throughout the whole transformation, a culture of enquiry and performance improvement will be fostered. The current processes for staff appraisal will be re-focused as a tool for enabling staff development.

The remaining component supports the exploitation of results in order to fuel a faster rate of improvement internally, whilst also building a reputation that is constantly being enhanced. This reputation becomes the external brand.

And that's it. Scores of individuals have discovered the benefit of ADVANCE to focus their thinking and development. As a result they have become more reflective, have greater self-awareness, they can demonstrate effective leadership in complex environments, and above all they achieve significant transformation for themselves and those around them.

Leading change in universities is challenging, but not impossible. Invest some time in your own development, listen to people and acquire your own coaching mindset, and you'll achieve far more than you ever imagined.

Good luck!

ABOUT THE AUTHOR

Richard Hill coaches Higher Education academics, researchers and managers so they can use data to remodel themselves, positively influence their environments, and become great leaders.

Starting life as an engineer, before studying computer science and becoming a university professor, Richard has held a number of management and senior leadership roles. Using over 20 years of industrial and academic experience, he helps people embrace change, showing academic leaders how to evaluate the strategic impact of learning, teaching and research.

His approach to organisational transformation is centred around the rigorous use of data to inform leadership development, and is the creator of the ADVANCE model for data-driven leadership.

Applying ADVANCE he transforms the performance of individuals and departments, achieving improved research productivity, superior teaching quality and higher student and staff achievement. Richard's academic writing workshops and academic culture change programmes inspire both junior and more established staff to develop external esteem and establish successful research careers.

For more information, visit www.datadrivenleader.com.